Find Your Purpose

Find Your Purpose

Build a better life and career

Kevan Hall

NICHOLAS BREALEY
PUBLISHING

London • Boston

First published by Nicholas Brealey Publishing in 2024
An imprint of John Murray Press

1

Copyright © Global Integration 2024

A CIP catalogue record for this title is available from the British Library

Trade Paperback ISBN 978 1 39981 279 5
ebook ISBN 978 1 39981 281 8

Typeset in Celeste by
Palimpsest Book Production Limited, Falkirk, Stirlingshire

Printed and bound in Great Britain by Clays Ltd, Elcograf S.p.A.

John Murray Press policy is to use papers that are natural, renewable
and recyclable products and made from wood grown in sustainable forests.
The logging and manufacturing processes are expected to conform
to the environmental regulations of the country of origin.

John Murray Press   Nicholas Brealey Publishing
Carmelite House   Hachette Book Group
50 Victoria Embankment   Market Place, Center 53, State Street
London EC4Y 0DZ   Boston, MA 02109, USA

www.nicholasbrealey.com

John Murray Press, part of Hodder & Stoughton Limited
An Hachette UK company

To my family who secretly enjoy and sometimes join my regular
experiments to try out new things in life

Contents

＠ ＠ ＠

Introduction

● ● ●

If you are reading this book, then it is likely that something has happened to interrupt the current flow of your life. This might have been driven by external factors, such as reaching a significant age milestone, becoming a parent or thinking about retirement. Or it could be driven by an internal realization that you have reached a stage where you want to take more control over your life and career.

We all go through different stages and make significant choices in our lives, and the decisions we make at these times determine the quality of the rest of our lives.

We are constantly making choices that take us down certain life and career paths and close other opportunities. But life does not come with an owner's manual on how to make these choices and many people just muddle through.

The purpose of this book is to give you the best tools and information to navigate important life choices, take control, and design a life and career of meaning, engagement and happiness.

People with a sense of purpose and meaning in life live longer, feel happier, enjoy better health, and are more engaged and productive at work. Applying these tools will help you design a more fulfilling career, enjoy your leisure time more, improve your relationships, and stay curious and open to learning new things.

This book came out of my attempt to find information and tools to help manage changes in my own life. I was starting to think about a life after full-time work and what that meant to my work, leisure and relationships.

I am a trainer with a passion for learning and a tendency to get carried away in research. My approach is to identify the best research, turn it into practical and actionable tools, and communicate and engage with people to discuss, refine and apply the techniques. I have done this successfully many times in my professional life so far, writing several business books, dozens of training courses and creating an organization that has trained over 150,000 people in more than 400 organizations around the world in leadership, collaboration, and personal effectiveness. Now it was time to turn my skills to developing myself.

I found a lot of great research into topics such as finding purpose, living a good life, creating engagement, designing your life for happiness and enjoyment and managing transitions. But there was nowhere that brought these insights together in a systematic, practical process. I ignored the anecdotal information or personal opinions that make up a lot of the self-help industry and most of the internet content and focused on ideas backed by credible research.

As a professional trainer I focused on selecting or developing the techniques that make these insights practical and actionable in real life. As I did the work myself and talked to others, I found that nearly everybody was looking for more purpose in life, particularly after their experiences during the pandemic period.

- Young people have been re-evaluating their relationship with work.

- People in their 30s and 40s have been looking for more purpose and work–life balance. Many chose to change jobs or careers in the 'great resignation'.

- People in their 50s and 60s have left the workforce in unprecedented numbers (although some are now drifting back).

- People in retirement have been rejecting the traditional model of gentle decline and seeking more active engagement with life.

Survey company Gallup found in 2022 that 65 per cent of people were re-evaluating the value of the parts of their lives outside work, 62 per cent longed for a bigger change in their life and 52 per cent were questioning the purpose of their work.

The pandemic seems to have triggered or accelerated a desire to find more purpose and meaning in life and has motivated many people to take a deeper look at what they want. In my own family, my son was in his 30s and re-evaluating his career, my daughter was coming towards the end of her second period of parental leave and thinking about the next stage of her life. My nephew was just starting his career in his first job and leaving home. Many of my friends were contemplating retirement and what that meant for their lives. Every time I spoke to somebody about managing the process of transition, it ended up being a lengthy and interesting conversation.

My motivation in writing this book is to help you take more control in managing your important life choices and transitions and to give you the information and tools to make informed choices that will have a positive impact on the rest of your life.

The choices will be yours, but you can be quite sure that others have gone through similar life stages before. There is an excellent chance that academics, thinkers and authors have studied these situations and can offer ideas and strategies that can help.

The quality of our lives lies in how we spend our time. Most of us spend about 40 per cent of our waking lives at work and another 25–40 per cent at leisure. If we are not engaged and fulfilled in these two areas, we have little chance of a happy life. However, to take just two examples that I will develop further later in the book, according to our research, only 20 per cent of people say they are highly engaged at work, while people spend an average of over 20 hours per week sitting passively in front of TV screens. It does not sound as though we are always getting the best out of our time.

Living a good life is about following your purpose, living according to your values, exercising your strengths and pursuing your passions. Unless you are extremely lucky you will not be able to do all of this in just one domain of your life. The trick is to find a balanced portfolio of activities that enables you to do all these things somewhere in your life and career.

Living a 'portfolio life' is about finding the right blend of career, leisure, interests and other activities that enable you to feel happy and fulfilled. It is also about how you do these things to build in enjoyment of the moment and improve the quality of the journey. This means that your unique portfolio needs to be driven by what gives you meaning. Nobody else can do it for you and nobody else can make the choices, and sometimes the sacrifices, necessary to make it a reality. This book is based firmly on the principle of you owning and driving the changes you want.

I also want to emphasize that this book is my perspective on the issues. I researched the topics extensively and looked for high-quality sources of information. However, inevitably the things that struck me as most useful were the things that resonate with my own life and experiences. You may come from a different demographic and have different experiences. I hope this book will add to the perspectives you bring and motivate you to seek out other sources of inspiration. I would love to hear about your experiences so I can learn from them too and I'll include some contact details at the end of the book.

The process and tool kit

My intent is to lead you through a systematic process with well-validated insights, tips, tools and techniques at each stage.

In the first part of the book I will give you a framework for designing a more fulfilling and engaging life to help you:

- understand the life transitions that most people go through and the critical decisions we make at these points

- identify the five key elements that bring wellbeing and happiness and how we can design them into how we live our lives

- define the six key areas we need to prioritize to build a good life.

I will then go on to show you how to be crystal clear about what gives meaning to your life:

- what you believe in – your values

- what you are good at – your strengths

- what you enjoy doing – your passions

- how to create a purpose statement.

These insights become an internal compass and a set of criteria for selecting the portfolio of activities that will give you a meaningful life and career.

In the later parts of the book I will apply some research-based techniques you can use to get the most out of your life in the key areas of living a good life:

- work, whether paid or unpaid

- leisure, hobbies and interests

- positive relationships

- lifelong learning

- a brief look at finance and health.

Lastly, I will introduce some techniques for creating an environment, habits and goals that will help you be much more likely to succeed in transforming the rest of your life.

Plan ahead, but not too far

Assuming you are old enough to look back 20 years, how different a person were you then? What were your opinions, perceptions and preoccupations? The chances are that you were a quite different person. Could you have known accurately who you would be today?

It is the same with the 'future you' – 20 years from now you will have had different experiences and will face different challenges and opportunities.

You may have read biographies or stories of people who knew their life path aged five and never deviated. These people are the tiny minority – for most of us life happens, we evolve and our track changes.

My advice in applying the exercises and ideas in this book is to use them to plan the next 5–10 years of your life, rather than the next 40 years. You will learn that some aspects of what give you meaning, such as your values, change slowly and will be a useful long-term guide. But the context in which you apply your values – for example at work, in leisure and in your relationships – will change over time. Rather than attempt an unrealistic and inflexible whole life plan, I would advise you to get started in what you think is the right direction and then learn, fine tune and course correct from time to time as life happens.

Successfully navigating key stages in your life is about making choices, exercising freedom and taking control. All of these require you to have the information and the tools to make the best choices.

Make a change

Some of the content of this book may genuinely drive major change in your life. Other parts are about incremental improvement – systematically building in more of the things you enjoy and cutting out the things that you do not. How you spend your time is the quality of your life, so if you can shift just 10 per cent of your work and leisure time from something that you do not actively enjoy to something that gives you more energy, then you make a significant improvement in the quality of your life. If you can make a 10 per cent improvement, why not 20 per cent?

I would love to hear about your experiences in applying the material in the book and any suggestions you have for improving it.

If you are someone who likes to learn by discussing things with a community of others going through a similar experience or would like support from expert trainers and coaches in these areas, you can find out about our live workshops, webinars, and coaching for individuals and for organizations at www.yourportfoliolife.com.

CHAPTER 1

Life Is in the Transitions

* * *

There are many life stages and events that people may experience that require us to revisit our perspectives and priorities. Here are a few common ones:

- young adulthood

- establishing or questioning your identity

- leaving home

- relocation

- parenthood

- gaining or losing a job

- moving house

- a new relationship, marriage, or divorce

- a major accident or illness

- mid-life changes

- reaching a significant age – 30, 40, 50, 60

- children leaving home

- major changes to your financial position

- loss of loved ones

- retirement

- ageing.

I have been through most of these myself, together with some less common ones like moving countries and starting my own business.

Sometimes a change in life can also be driven by an internal revelation, a desire to take control, solve a difficult situation or revitalise aspects of your life. In my case, starting my own business for example was driven by the desire for autonomy, which is one of my core values.

In fact, there are so many transitions, and they are such significant moments in our lives, that it might be more accurate to say that our lives are about our transitions, with occasional moments of stability in between for us to catch our breath!

The Hindu tradition identifies four key life stages with different areas of focus:

1. Up to age 25: the scholar – learning, finding identity, leaving home.

2. To 55: the householder – earning a living, building a family, achieving.

3. To 75: retreat or retirement – contemplation, focusing on the welfare of the community and self-development.

4. 75-plus: preparing for death, passing on your wisdom and the meaning of life.

These stages see a steadily broadening frame of reference from focusing on yourself as an individual to family and then to the wider community and the universe.

At each stage of life, we confront new questions and learn new lessons, which lead to more questions and further transitions:

- In childhood we ask: who am I?

- In adolescence: what do I want to be when I grow up?

- As a young adult: what is my calling?

- In mid-life: what is it all about?

- In older adulthood: how do I age and grow?

Because of this you have already learned a few skills and some things about yourself that will help you with the next stage. What are the major transitions that you have navigated already and what did you learn from each of them?

My major transitions	What did I learn?

Given how regular and important these life transitions are, it is surprising how little advice and support we get in navigating these important moments. The decisions we make at these times determine the quality of the rest of our lives.

Today these life transitions are getting even more diverse and complex.

- **People are living longer and in better health.** Children born in the early 2020s in the UK are expected to live on average to age 90, so it would be prudent for them to plan on a 100-year life. The impact of both our good and bad decisions, particularly those we make early in life, is much greater when compounded over 100 years rather than 70. Increasing longevity means that people will either choose to or need to work for longer and will have much longer periods in retirement when they are in good health. The UK, Denmark, Poland, Canada, Australia, New Zealand and the United States already have laws banning mandatory retirement. Expect more to follow.

- **The nature of work is changing fast.** The accelerating rate of technological change means that skills will become out of date much more quickly and people should expect to retrain significantly more than once during their careers. Careers are unlikely to be a linear progression up a clearly defined ladder. Increases in freelancing and the gig economy mean that fewer individuals will rely on a single employer.

  New technologies such as artificial intelligence (AI) are likely to replace some jobs entirely. PricewaterhouseCoopers, a consulting organization, forecast in 2018 that AI will create more new jobs than it displaces (just like many previous waves of technology-driven change). Many more roles will be in new areas or augmented by technology to provide faster and better information and decision support. While writing this book it was announced that AI natural language processing tools would be incorporated into Microsoft Bing and Office and Google Search. This will rapidly accelerate the adoption of AI into everyday tasks and transform the world of work.

  Since the rise of remote working during the pandemic period, many more jobs can now be done from any location. Our choices about work are less constrained by where we live, meaning more major life choices are available with the opportunity to work from anywhere. People seem to be giving more priority to finding a sense of purpose and happiness at work and are more willing to change jobs in search of it.

- **There is a greater diversity in family units, relationships and identity.** The structure of families is changing from the traditional nuclear family of 50 years ago. Fewer people are getting married, more are getting divorced, and they are having fewer children later. There are more dual-career, single-parent and single-person households. There is greater recognition of the spectrum of gender identity and understanding of different types of relationships.

- **There is more free time.** In addition to a longer retirement, many people are experiencing longer periods of leisure or other unstructured time. Leisure takes up 25–40 per cent of people's waking time in developed economies. Experiments in flexible working, four-day weeks and universal basic income are the beginning of a general reduction in the amount of time most people spend at work. Without this structure, people will be free to make choices about how they spend a much bigger proportion of their time. However, we are never really taught to use our leisure time well. We could use this time to learn and grow or experience variety, or we could sit passively in front of a screen.

The fact that we are living longer and in better health means that we will have even more transitions to navigate. The increase in work, leisure and lifestyle options means that, at each stage of our lives, we will have a much greater range of choices than those faced by previous generations.

As we have more freedom to make a wider variety of choices over a longer period, we have an increasing need to be able to make smart and informed decisions about our future direction. At the same time there may be few role models or well-trodden pathways to follow as we make choices that were not common, or even imagined, in previous generations.

Navigating life transitions

'Change is situational, transition is psychological. It is not the events; it is the inner reorientation and self-redefinition you have to go through in order to incorporate those changes into your life. Without a transition, change is just a rearrangement of the furniture.'

William Bridges, *Transitions: Making Sense of Life's Changes*

Change is something that can happen to you, for good or ill. You could win the lottery or lose your job. Transition may be triggered by external changes or it could be stimulated by internal changes and ideas. The outer change can happen very quickly, the inner usually takes much longer.

Transition is about how you deal with these changes and is therefore within your control. Nobody else can transition for you. As a result, the process of transition is often either guided or obstructed by our inner drivers and thoughts about the situation.

Life transitions tend to go through some predictable stages.

1 LETTING GO OF THE OLD

Transitions often start when we become aware of some significant change in life. This might be something we have actively chosen, such as getting married or becoming a new parent, or something that happens to us, such as an accident or losing a job.

In positive change there are things to look forward to, but even then there are aspects of the previous stage that we are concerned about losing. We may experience some resistance, even grieving for some aspects of the previous stage of our lives. For example, we may be looking forward to our kids leaving home but dreading it at the same time.

This is not unusual, but it is good to admit this to ourselves, take a balanced view of the net benefit of the change and think through how we preserve as best we can the things we enjoyed from the previous stage. We may not have as much time for our friends once we start work, for example, but we do want to find a way to maintain those relationships.

At every transition we experience gains and losses. We give up some of our old options and gain others. Think about the current or next transition stage that you are experiencing or likely to experience. How are you thinking and feeling about the positives and negatives of this next stage?

Complete the table with your thoughts about the positives and negatives as you see them now.

What do you see as the negatives of the transition, what will you be giving up?	What do you see as the positives of the situation, what will you be gaining?

- What is the balance of the language and sentiment you have captured here – positive or negative?

- For important things you feel you are losing, have you considered the potential this creates for a new positive?

- What can you do to accentuate the positives of the new situation?

- What do you want to make sure you carry forward into the next stage?

- What is it time to let go of in your life right now?

You might find it useful to think back to other transitions you have been through in the same way to reflect on what you learned and the balance of benefits you gained from the change. This is part of the process of acknowledging the good things about your previous life stage and, where appropriate, either letting them go or building them into the next stage of your life.

2 SIT WITH THE UNCERTAINTY

Going through a major change in life can cause uncertainty. It would be surprising if it did not.

One of the skills of successfully managing a transition is being prepared to sit with a period of uncertainty for a while. Do not be tempted to rush ahead too fast and block out the possibilities you could be considering at this stage in search of quick stability – you will regret it in the long term.

It is also a good time to do your research. In Chapter 8, you will see some tips and ideas on how to stimulate your curiosity and access information. Buying this book is a great start.

In the academic research, this stage is often called a 'liminal space'. It is where you start to disengage from the old but have not yet embraced the new. You are at the threshold, but you have not entered the new stage yet.

Once you embrace your new role and identity, you will have either consciously or unconsciously blocked out a lot of options. Take the time to really think through what you want from the next stage of your life. Expect this to feel uncomfortable but be prepared to live with it for a while to allow time for more considered decisions.

Your destination will not be clear at this stage. You will have questions to ask and choices to make. In this book, I will take you back to some fundamentals, your values, your passions, your natural strengths and your purpose. Make sure you do these exercises before you start to make significant choices about the future. Understanding these internal drivers should provide you with guidelines on what kinds of solutions are likely to give you meaning and make you feel fulfilled. They will help you rule out some options and pay more attention to others.

This is a good time to try some experiments. If you have ideas about how you would like your life to be, can you test them out? The purpose of an experiment is to learn – we test our hypothesis or idea and look for evidence. If the experiment works out and we enjoy the experience, then it might be something we want to build on. If it does not, we have learned something valuable that will help us design our next experiment.

It can also be valuable to talk to other people who have been through a similar experience. Look for people who have had a positive experience as they have done a good job of navigating the change.

You will find lots of exercises and ideas in the rest of this book on how you can actively and intentionally redesign your work, leisure, relationships and learning for the next stage of your life.

3 EMBRACE THE NEW AND BE READY TO EVOLVE

As your direction becomes clearer you will feel a mental shift as you start to commit to the future. This happens more easily once you have identified a future that is in some ways better than your past.

Traditional societies have formal 'rites of passage' celebrating, for example, the transition to adulthood. Think about how we celebrate graduation, naming ceremonies, weddings and other formal life transitions. These events are partly about recognition and celebration and partly about a public affirmation in front of family and friends that you are moving on to the next stage.

How could you celebrate and recognize the new stage you are moving on to? Is there an excuse for a party? One of the things my son-in-law noticed when he joined our family was how often we celebrated things. He would joke, 'It's Thursday, get the champagne out.' Celebration tends to bring out positive feelings and recognize that something is important (and Thursdays are extremely important).

We also need to get a sense of balance about how much change we are going through. It is rare that everything changes at once, so it can be a useful strategy to keep some familiar routines in place to give a sense of continuity and to allow time to focus on a few important new areas you are trying to work on.

In real life of course we do not always proceed in a nice, neat order – you may move through the process at different speeds in different parts of your life, and sometimes you will need to cycle back.

How quickly we move through this process may be a function of personality, with some people who are comfortable with change being quicker to adapt to the new than others. It may also be a function of how much choice you are able to exercise depending on your personal circumstances.

Be prepared to let your approach evolve as you learn and experience more. Keep some space for continued experiments and for reflection on how it is going and how you can improve the experience.

The middle of transitions is when it feels most destabilizing. This is precisely because this is the time when we have the most freedom and choice. Freedom can be frightening, particularly if we do not have the information to make good decisions.

- The number one source of transition stress is not having prepared – so prepare.

- Having a sense of control over events is important, so focus on what you can control during times of uncertainty. In general, this means focusing on yourself, your attention and your attitude.

- Build the knowledge and skills you need for the transition and your next life stage. For example, if your next life stage is parenting, there are some predictable challenges coming your way and no shortage of advice.

- Reflect on what gives you meaning and enjoyment and build even more of that into the next stage of your life.

- Make conscious decisions and plans; do not just drift into a future you do not necessarily want.

- Take your time.

That is the kind of person I am – the identity trap

To become something else you need to stop being at least part of what you are now.

I had an international corporate career; I founded my own business and spent 30 years growing it. Work was and still is a big piece of how I spend my time and where I get a lot of my identity from. As I started to think about a life beyond full-time work, I decided to take a day a week to sample different activities.

As an academically bright student, I had been steered away from practical subjects, yet I really enjoyed my experiences of blacksmithing, woodturning, glassblowing and carving. I was told at school that I was 'not very good' at languages and art. Yet when I moved to France, I learned the language quite quickly (although with an entertaining

Yorkshire accent apparently) and when I took up drawing, I was good at it.

I learned that the process of building your identity, especially in early life, was a process of closing off options. In adolescence, as we start to create our sense of self and identity, we become the 'kind of person' who likes certain subjects at school and dislikes others. We associate with a particular lifestyle group – as a nerd, a sports jock, a music lover. We become the kind of person who likes some things and dislikes others and this helps us distinguish ourselves from other groups. We have all seen groups of teenagers who insist on signalling their unique identity by choosing to dress the same way as all their friends.

As we get older, we play certain roles at work, and increasingly define ourselves by the type of person we 'are'. We move beyond identifying ourselves as part of groups and search for more of a unique identity that reflects the complexity of our lives. We become the kind of person who drives a certain car, lives in a certain area, enjoys specific types of food, dislikes some kinds of music, clothes or sports, enjoys particular types of vacations, only reads certain authors, and so forth.

Think about how you introduce yourself to someone new and what information you give about yourself. Often people are looking for information that allows them to pigeon-hole you, particularly in terms of where you sit in the status pecking order.

In the UK, once you can get a sense for where people live, the kind of job they have, the car they drive and their hobbies you can start to infer an awful lot more about them. It can be an entertaining game to not give any of this kind of information about yourself when you meet someone new. You normally find that people get quite uncomfortable after a while of being unable to slot you into the way they categorize the world.

What kind of person are you?

- Cats or dogs

- Sporty or academic

- Action movies or romance

- Outdoor or indoor

- Thinker or doer

- Lover or fighter

- Football or tennis.

Try it for yourself: **I am the kind of person who...**

Likes	Dislikes

Now ask yourself: **what does this stop me doing?** Do these beliefs I have about myself serve me well or do they get in the way of my experiences? What would I do differently if I explored all these potential choices rather than just half of them?

You can imagine the process of creating an identity as a narrowing slice of a pie chart. When you are very young you have the potential to have almost any identity. You are then shaped by your culture, your family, your teachers, your peers and your own choices. These choices give structure to your life and define your identity, but they also tend to exclude you from other potential options.

Eventually we live our life in a very constrained slice of the pie chart because that is the 'kind of person we are'. This can be very comfortable, but it sure does exclude a lot of options.

At major transition points we can challenge these self-imposed limitations. Losing a job may open up career choices you never would have thought about; becoming a parent may reveal aspects of your character you have never exercised before.

For many people, work is an important source of identity, to the extent that retired people may still describe themselves relative to their

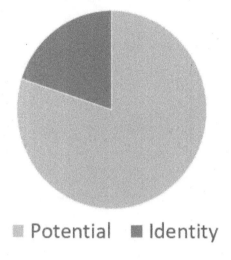

■ Potential   ■ Identity

former role: 'I am a retired teacher.' The loss of that identity for some can feel like falling off a cliff. The more successful your career, the more likely you are to feel the loss of identity in retirement.

As a thought experiment, imagine that all the people on earth disappear, except for you. All the things are still here, but none of the people. Imagine, in this situation, how would you choose to spend your time, where would you go, what car would you drive, what hobbies and activities would you follow, would you dress for fashion or comfort?

As you think through your life in this world, you may find some things do not change. I would still choose to drive a fast car because I love driving. But would you dress fashionably if there were nobody there to see it? Most people come to realize that many of the things they do are about status or because of how other people might view them.

Some start to imagine how their priorities might be different in the next stage of their lives if they lived life for what gives them meaning rather than what other people might think.

It may not be until retirement that we have a genuine option to reject the expectations we have built up throughout our lives and rediscover other parts of our potential identity. Here are some questions to consider:

- Does the transition you are going through threaten a part of your identity?

- Does it challenge your beliefs about the kind of person you are?

- Does it bring opportunities to express underdeveloped parts of your identity?

- Are there parts of your old identity that you are keen to move on from?

- Are there things you loved in the past that you can rediscover in this next stage?

I hope at this stage that you realize that going through life transitions is normal and that you are not alone. I also hope you are open to some uncertainty and some personal reinvention and are prepared to give this some time before you jump into important decisions.

In the next three chapters I will look at how we can design more engagement and happiness into the key areas of our lives and start to base our lives and careers around what gives us real meaning.

CHAPTER 2

The Pursuit of Happiness

● ● ●

As we think about improving our life, it inevitably leads to the question: What is the meaning of my life?

I will lead you through some exercises in the next chapters to help you discover your personal values, strengths, passions and purpose. Whatever gives you meaning is up to you, but your choice will shape your life. Popular choices around the meaning of life include:

1. Happiness (normally at the top of the list.)

2. Family

3. Giving something back

4. Material success

5. Your relationship with something greater than yourself – spirituality

6. Inner harmony and acceptance

7. The number 42 (if you are not a fan of *The Hitchhiker's Guide to the Galaxy*, look it up).

Conventional wisdom is that your purpose needs to include a connection to something more than just yourself to bring about true happiness. The nature of this connection is often influenced by culture. A lot of US-based writers insist you can only find meaning through your relationship with your God. Buddhists may emphasize personal spirituality and your connection with the universe. Japanese examples are often more focused on your place within a community.

I do not intend to be prescriptive about this, but to help you work out what this is for yourself. Nobody else can tell you what gives you meaning. Whatever we are seeking – power, money, spiritual enlightenment – it is probably because we think it will make us happy.

Famously, the US constitution elevates the pursuit of happiness to an inalienable right on a par with the right to life and liberty:

> *'We hold these truths to be sacred & undeniable; that all men are created equal and independent, that from that equal creation they derive rights inherent & inalienable, among which are the preservation of life, & liberty, & the pursuit of happiness.'*

So how do we pursue happiness?

Happiness from material success

A lot of people live their lives as if they believe that material success is the route to happiness.

As a young man starting my career in the 'greed is good' London of the 1980s, I remember with a certain level of fondness a sticker in the back window of a Ferrari saying, 'He who dies with the most toys wins'. It seemed like a good ethos to someone in their early 20s starting out with nothing.

The risk of materialism as a goal, of course, is that it assumes that happiness will come from the next material thing – whether that be a handbag, a car, a house, the latest phone or the next promotion. When inevitably this does not make you happy for long, there is always a more expensive option to aim for. We can easily live our lives on a hamster wheel chasing after the next shiny new thing.

At the same time, by constantly assuming that happiness lies in the next thing we tend to neglect the present moment, which is where happiness really happens.

Aspiring to a specific material possession will bring only very short-lived happiness.

We have all experienced it ourselves. We had a positive experience such as moving house or a pay rise and we felt happy for a while, but after a time this became the norm and we went back to our normal level of happiness. This effect is sometimes called the hedonistic treadmill. The new situation becomes the norm, we cease to get a positive happiness effect from it and we return to our normal 'happiness set point'.

There is no denying that money can be helpful – there is an old saying that 'money does not solve all your problems, but it does solve all of your money problems'. Wealthy people live significantly longer and in better health than poorer people and have lower rates of cancer and obesity. They also experience lower rates of age-related cognitive degeneration.

However, we also hear from the Bible that 'money is the root of all evil' and even 'it is easier for a camel to go through the eye of a needle than for someone who is rich to enter the kingdom of God', which seems a bit harsh. We are clearly conflicted about the impact of wealth.

Being in poverty correlates with a lot of things that make us unhappy and unhealthy. It also reduces choices, and having control over your life is a crucial element of happiness. But the research shows that money only helps up to a point, then diminishing returns set in.

In a 2013 study by Elizabeth Dunn and Michael Norton, people with a middle-class standard of living were found to be happier than people who lived in poverty. However, in the US, beyond an income of $75,000 per year, happiness did not increase. At the time of writing that is equivalent to about $100,000 per year – quite a high level (only 5 per cent of earners in the UK earn more than this per year).

Later studies found, unsurprisingly, that the level at which more money correlated with more happiness peaked at different places depending on the cost of living where the research was done. They also found that how you earned the money was important – for example, clergy on lower salaries were happier than lawyers earning significantly more.

Dunn, Aknin and Norton also found that it was important what you spent that wealth on. More material possessions generated a lot less happiness than a focus on experiences, especially if those experiences were shared with someone else. They also found that generosity had an even more significant impact; buying less for yourself and more for others generated more happiness.

So, in general, it is better for your happiness to be well off than to be poor, but pursuing improvements to our material circumstances will have relatively little impact on our happiness in the long term.

Happiness from inner serenity

There are, of course, traditions that reject external factors and insist that happiness can only come from within. Buddhist thinking makes a compelling case that all suffering comes from attachment or striving for something more. Buddhists propose that true happiness comes from acceptance, connecting with your inner self and learning to live mindfully in the moment.

Mindfulness is a powerful counter to the practice of always striving for the next thing. It is healthy both mentally and physically to appreciate the present moment and enjoy the now. If we can focus on the present moment, then enjoyment often happens naturally.

Buddhists would say that you can still achieve success by being mindful because it makes you more centred, open to the universe and more receptive to opportunities. Acceptance and inner harmony do not need to mean you do not have an intent to improve, but success is more about self-development and enlightenment rather than seeking material acquisition.

It is self-evidently true that only the present moment exists to enjoy. The past cannot be changed and we tend to see it through an imperfect filter of recollection – the future is imaginary until it becomes the present.

There is a lot of wisdom in the Japanese phrase *ichigo ichie*: 'in this moment, an opportunity'. It encourages us to treat every experience as if it will never happen again. Every moment is unique and will never be repeated in the same way, so we need to be open to enjoying each unique moment before it inevitably slips away.

Meditation helps with depression and is recognized by UK health authorities as at least as effective as drugs or therapy. It has also been found to reduce stress, cortisol (a stress hormone), inflammation and some age-related brain changes. A 2013 meta-analysis of 209 studies on meditation concluded that mindfulness-based therapy is an effective treatment for a variety of psychological problems and is especially effective for reducing anxiety, depression and stress.

Meditation also seems to help in dealing with chronic pain. Practitioners report that it reduces feelings of unpleasantness and improves mood and quality of life.

Becoming more mindful and appreciating the present moment has an important part to play in a happy life. You will easily find online a range of simple apps and audio books that will help you give meditation and mindfulness a go.

Your happiness setpoint

In her book *The How of Happiness*, researcher Sonja Lyubomirsky studies why different people feel different levels of happiness. She then identifies scientifically validated actions we can take to increase our happiness. She talks about each of us having a different 'happiness setpoint', a normal level of happiness that represents a baseline which we are likely to come back to after either positive or negative experiences.

Some good news is that the natural happiness setpoint on average is positive – 75 per cent of people are more happy than unhappy.

A study by Brickman and Campbell in 1971 even found that there was little long-term difference in happiness between people who had won large amounts of money on the lottery and people who had been paralysed in accidents. Both returned to their previous levels of happiness.

It is reassuring that as we adapt equally to negative circumstances, these do not necessarily need to cause a long-term reduction in happiness.

From studies of twins, Lyubomirsky in *The How of Happiness* found that 50 per cent of the differences in happiness between people was based on genetics. Some people are born with a higher predisposition to happiness than others.

Please note that this is not an excuse to be miserable because 'it is in my genes'. Genes do not cause or determine happiness or unhappiness; they just predispose us in that direction. We can still improve our happiness levels through our actions and attitudes.

The next 10 per cent of the difference in happiness between individuals was determined by life circumstances such as wealth, health, physical appearance and marital status. Given the small impact these things have on our happiness, it is surprising how much time we spend obsessing over things like wealth and possessions. The reality is that these factors usually cause only a short-term change in happiness before we return to our normal setpoint.

The remaining 40 per cent of the difference in happiness between individuals was caused by our behaviours and daily activities, what we do and how we are thinking about our everyday lives.

By incorporating these insights, we can intentionally raise and sustain a higher happiness setpoint.

Later research has criticized the conveniently round numbers in this research but confirmed that each of these factors has an important influence.

Five ways to flourish

The most compelling research I found on happiness came from Martin Seligman. Seligman is a rigorous academic, a former president of the American Psychological Association and a professor of psychology at the University of Pennsylvania. His book *Flourish* is a must-read.

He became disillusioned with psychology's preoccupation with abnormal behaviour and unhappiness and pioneered the idea of positive psychology. He originally researched the sources of happiness, but then extended his interest to the broader concept of wellbeing. He found that wellbeing on its own cannot easily be defined or measured, so he broke it down into five independent elements that can be measured and improved. He proposed that, given a free choice, people would pursue each of these five elements for its own sake:

1. The search for meaning

2. Positive relationships

3. Positive emotions

4. Accomplishment

5. Engagement.

When I first found his work, he was focusing just on the top three as important elements of happiness. I always felt it was missing something about getting things done. When he added accomplishment and engagement, it completed the picture.

THE SEARCH FOR MEANING

This is usually held to be about serving something you think is bigger than yourself – family, community, society, planet. But fundamentally it is about whatever gives meaning to you, so it is deeply personal.

In Chapter 3, I will lead you through a process for understanding and capturing your values, passions, strengths and purpose – the key elements that define meaning in your life. Through the exercises in the other areas of building a meaningful life, such as in our work, our leisure, our learning and our relationships, I will help you select more meaningful activities and build more meaning into everything you do.

POSITIVE RELATIONSHIPS

The Harvard Study of Adult Development studied 724 men over 75 years and the central finding was that the most important factor in continued health and wellbeing was good relationships. The researchers found that 'people who are more socially connected to family, to friends and to community are happier, healthier, and live longer than people who are less well connected'.

It is not the number of friends but the quality of your closest relationship that counts. In Chapter 6, I will help you analyse the quality of your relationships and work on improving the ones you want to.

POSITIVE EMOTIONS

It seems self-evident that happiness is associated with positive emotions such as pleasure, joy, warmth and comfort. However, some of these things are easy to shortcut by doing things that give short-term pleasure but cause longer-term problems.

The trick in increasing happiness is to magnify the positive emotions by practising positive behaviours more often. This comes from learning to notice and enjoy them more intensely as they happen and reflecting on them afterwards to intensify the benefit we get from the experience.

Here are four practical areas you can work on:

- **Kindness.** In Seligman's studies, doing a kindness for someone else produced the single most reliable increase in wellbeing of any exercise he tested. It almost does not matter what the kindness is, just do something nice for someone else and you will see the benefit in your own happiness.

We can train ourselves to look for opportunities to make small acts of kindness throughout the day in the way we interact with people and the things we do. It could be the way we treat people at the coffee shop, small acts of charity or looking for opportunities to be helpful to people. Once you prime yourself to look for opportunities, you will find them more often. Do not make this a chore or a formal target of 'nine compulsory acts of charity a week', try to make it spontaneous and vary what you do, or it will become habitual and you will lose the benefit.

- **Gratitude and appreciation.** We can increase our sense of wellbeing by being thankful for what we have. Cultivating gratitude is about regularly thinking about and remembering to focus on things we are grateful for and appreciate in our lives.

  Rather than wait for something particularly positive to happen, why not just sit down and count your blessings? What and who are you grateful for or appreciate in your life? For a bonus, tell the people you are grateful to that you appreciate how they make you feel.

  Another good practice is to keep a gratitude journal, where you reflect at the end of each week and capture at least three good things that happened that week. The research found that for most people, doing this once a week was about right; if you tried to do it every day it lost some of its impact.

  We can also learn to make the everyday moments of pleasure more explicit. If anything delights you, no matter how small, notice it and say aloud how good it is. By paying more attention to the positive moments you will notice more of them in your life.

- **Savouring.** When we savour something, we intentionally seek to extend or increase the pleasure of a current or past experience by focusing on it or revisiting it. It might be savouring the present moment by focusing on the experience intently, such as when you enjoy a great meal, or it could be mentally revisiting past events to enjoy them again. Savouring the positive experiences in our life has been shown to increase happiness over and above the positive feelings caused by the initial event.

  It is human nature to spend more time thinking about what went badly than about what went well. We can counteract that by spending some time actively focusing on the positives. To savour a past event, simply put aside some time to sit down and recall the event in detail. Try to remember vividly how the situation engaged each of your senses. Allow the experience to stretch out in time and enjoy the events and feelings again. Your brain struggles to tell the difference between something that really happened and a strong emotional reflection like this, so you get the benefits of the positive emotions a second time. Repeat as needed, and do not forget to look out for, or plan to have more of, the experiences you savour the most.

You can also help trigger savouring in other people. When someone you know tells you some good news, respond actively and constructively. Congratulate them, ask for more details of what happened and how that made them feel. Let them know you think they deserve it.

- **Optimism.** It is our hopefulness and confidence about the future. Seligman noticed that when optimists and pessimists experience something they tend to interpret them differently in three major areas:

  - Permanence – do I think the situation is going to last for ever?
  - Pervasiveness – does it affect many areas of my life or is it just something specific?
  - Personalization – to what extent have I caused the situation?

Optimists tend to think difficult things are short-lived, specific to that context and caused by external events. Pessimists think the same event is going to last for ever, will have an impact on all areas of their life and that they personally caused it to happen. Research has shown that optimists have lower mortality and heart disease, faster walking speed, lower levels of depression, better resistance to colds and better coping skills. Optimistic people also tend to take a more proactive approach to health and lifestyle.

How do you tend to react to and interpret events? If you would like to make a change in this area, you might find the book *Learned Optimism* by Martin Seligman a useful read.

A good way to exercise your optimism is to spend some time imagining your best possible future self. What would you be doing? How would you behave and how would you be thinking?

If you visualize this future self vividly enough it will start to influence your current behaviour.

It is important to keep mixing up the things you do in these four areas – if you do the same thing every time it just becomes part of your routine and you start to lose the benefits. Try out a variety of ways of doing a kindness, showing gratitude, savouring your experiences and showing optimism.

Physical exercise also helps generate positive emotions. It is particularly good to spend time in nature and more vigorous exercise generates an improvement in mood. A study by Karmel Choi, a clinical and research fellow at the Harvard T.H. Chan School of Public Health, found a 26 per cent decrease in the odds of becoming depressed for each major increase in physical activity', for example replacing 15 minutes of sitting with 15 minutes of running, or one hour of sitting with one hour of moderate activity like brisk walking.

It is the little things that cause positive emotions, not the big-ticket lottery wins or a new house, so invest in a stream of positive experiences and responses over time to create sustained happiness.

One thing that does not help in generating positive emotions is making social comparisons. Happy people care less about such things and evaluate their success by their own internal factors. They take pleasure in others' successes.

ACCOMPLISHMENT

Accomplishment is about success, however you define it. When we feel we are winning, achieving and mastering something for its own sake, we tend to feel good.

Understanding what gives meaning to you will bring you some powerful indicators of what accomplishments are likely to feel the best. Accomplishing something that is consistent with your values and purpose is an important part of a happy life.

Later chapters will help you define what you want to accomplish in your work, leisure, relationships, learning and general wellbeing. The section on action planning will give some structure for how to organize yourself to maximize the chances of you accomplishing what you set out to achieve.

If you are approaching retirement, this can be something to think about carefully. In a traditional work career, we are used to meeting organizational goals and having our achievements appraised and measured by other people's standards. We are recognized and rewarded by organizational status and money. These external measures and validations can disappear in retirement, so it is important that we define what we want to achieve from our activity, which could involve work of a different type and a bigger range of leisure activities. I will come back to these themes later in the book.

What gives you a sense of accomplishment?

ENGAGEMENT

Seligman associates engagement with the idea of 'flow'. Flow is that intrinsically rewarding experience when you are 'in the zone', completely absorbed in what you are doing. You are exercising your strengths and overcoming challenges. You know you are in flow when you do not notice the time.

As Mihaly Csikszentmihalyi, the Hungarian-American psychologist, wrote in *Flow: The Psychology of Optimal Experience*, 'The best moments in our lives are not the passive, receptive, relaxing times . . . The best moments usually occur if a person's body or mind is stretched to its limits in a voluntary effort to accomplish something difficult and worthwhile.'

I am going to go into much more detail on the concept of flow and how to design it into your work and leisure activities later in Chapter 4.

Happiness and age

There is good evidence that happiness on average tends to improve after middle age. A UK Office for National Statistics report covering over 300,000 adults between 2012 and 2015 found:

- those aged 65–79 reported the highest levels of wellbeing

- ratings of life satisfaction and happiness were at their lowest for those aged 45–59

- although wellbeing did then decline for the over-75 group, up to their 90s they were still happier than people in their middle years

- most of the fall for these older groups came from a reduction in their feeling that the activities they do in life are worthwhile, so a strong sense of meaning is important even at this age.

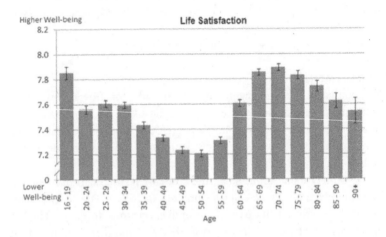

Graph data from Measuring National Wellbeing: At what age is personal wellbeing the highest? Annual Population Survey 2016, Office for National Statistics licensed under the Open Government Licence v.3.0

If you are in early middle-age, do not worry, it does get better. By the time you reach your early 70s, the chances are you will be happier than you ever were.

If you are in your 20s or 30s, your life is likely to become more complicated in the next decades, with a broader range of responsibilities and pressures. Because of this, it is even more important for you to take on board these techniques for engineering happiness into your life to help compensate for the other elements that will come along and get in the way.

Whatever we are seeking – power, money or spiritual enlightenment – it is probably because we think it will make us happy.

The research on happiness has given us some clear elements to pursue as we design the various aspects of our life. In the rest of the book, I will show you how to systematically design these elements into your leisure, your work, your relationships, your learning and other aspects of your life.

WHAT MAKES A GOOD LIFE?

When you start thinking about building a better life, you must prioritize. It is a big subject and could involve almost any topic you can imagine.

I wanted to identify the key areas where improvements could have the most impact on our lives and careers. There is extensive research from around the world into which elements of life tend to lead to happiness and fulfilment. I surveyed over 50 books and academic papers on this subject. They spanned a wide range of areas, from the study of success and longevity to happiness and life coaching, and I identified the elements that were mentioned the most often.

These elements will provide a framework for the rest of the book. In each of these areas I will propose some ideas and tools you can use to re-engineer your life for increased engagement and happiness.

THE ELEMENTS OF A GOOD LIFE

1. **Finding meaning and purpose.** A good life has some point to it; it involves living in a way that is consistent with your values, exercising your strengths, pursuing your passions and moving towards a purpose.

2. **Meaningful 'work'.** Whether paid or unpaid, work is about staying active and achieving something that has meaning to you. It is also about being engaged and enjoying the process of doing the work.

3. **Engaging leisure and interests.** Most people aspire to more leisure. Living a fulfilled life includes finding the right balance of relaxation, fun, hobbies and interests that enable us to be both relaxed and engaged.

4. **Positive relationships.** The quantity and quality of meaningful relationships in your life is a major factor in health and happiness.

5. **Lifelong learning.** The curiosity and ability to continue to learn new things, thrive and grow as a person.

6. **Physical and mental health and wellbeing.**

7. **Financial wellbeing.**

This short chapter includes a high-level audit in each of these elements and encourages you to prioritize where you will focus your efforts as you work through the exercises in the rest of the book.

Your satisfaction and priorities will change over time, particularly when you go through major life transitions. You can come back to this chapter from time to time to re-evaluate your satisfaction with each of the essential elements of a good life.

Developing your best life and career means finding the variety and balance of life and work activities that meet your values and purpose and allow you to exercise your skills. You do not have to meet all your values in one area. For example, if one of your values is creativity but you work in a job that does not require much of this, you may balance this with creative hobbies and interests. The important thing is that across all these seven areas your full range of values, strengths, passions and purpose is expressed in a way that leaves you feeling fulfilled.

You are unlikely to be surprised by this list of key areas to focus on, it is obvious. If you think there is something missing that is essential to your life, feel free to add it to the list below. However, beware of all prescriptions telling you what 'should' be important in your life (even the ones in this book), it is your unique life so feel free to shape it around the things you think are important.

If there are some of these elements that you do not think are important to you, just be careful to check you have not neglected them for so long that you have convinced yourself they do not matter. It might be worth doing a couple of experiments to see if engaging in these areas enriches your life.

What does make a difference is **systematically working to improve your life in each area**. It provides a framework and helps us prioritize.

Later in this book you will find ideas and exercises to work on in each of these areas, but you can start now with a quick, high-level self-assessment of where you are now. First impressions are often accurate – after all, we are each of us the world expert in our own lives. Feel free to add anything you believe is essential to your fulfilment or happiness that is not captured by these categories.

	What is the priority of each area for you?	How satisfied are you with each of these areas on a scale of 1–10?	Why did you give that satisfaction score? Where do you need to improve?
1. Finding meaning and purpose.			
2. Meaningful 'work'.			
3. Lifelong learning.			
4. Engaging leisure and interests.			
5. Positive relationships.			
6. Physical and mental health and wellbeing.			
7. Financial wellbeing.			

In this book we will spend most of our time on segments 1 to 5.

- In physical and mental health and wellbeing I will share some general principles, but my experience is that most people already know how to live a life of relative wellbeing in these areas: controlling your weight, eating a healthy diet, taking regular exercise, not smoking, getting enough sleep, spending time in nature, learning to deal with stress, etc. The challenge is not in knowing what to do, it is in doing it. I will not be going into these topics in detail as there is a wealth of other advice and expertise available in these areas. I will, however, restate some basic principles and you can work on applying them through the action planning part of this book.

• In financial wellbeing there are many extremely specific resources and advisors and the suitability of these varies widely by country and tax system. There are also tight regulatory requirements on offering specific advice. In the UK, for example, 90 per cent of people retire with a financial plan, but only 10 per cent have a plan for how they will spend their time in these other areas. In this critical area I will share some general principles and encourage you to take professional advice.

You could choose to go straight to the chapters that focus on your highest priorities at this point, but I would strongly recommend you start with Chapter 3, as this is fundamental to making good choices in the other areas and I will often refer in later chapters to the work you do there.

I will encourage you at the end of the book to set aside time to regularly review your progress in each of these areas to make sure you are constantly moving in the direction of the life you want.

CHAPTER 3

Finding Your Unique Purpose and Meaning

* * *

To design a more fulfilling and engaging life we need to understand what gives us meaning and enjoyment. To do this we will start by helping you understand your values, passions, strengths and purpose.

Asking someone to define the purpose of their life is a huge question. In our training we have found it is better to start by coming at it from two or three different directions before attempting to bring it all together into a purpose statement.

In this chapter we are going to examine what brings meaning to life in three key areas:

- Our values – what we believe in

- Our passions – what we love doing

- Our strengths – what we are good at and enjoy.

Once we have done this we will come back to the sweet spot where all three of these intersect and each of them should give us some clues to our purpose.

Once we understand our values, passions, strengths and purpose we will have created an internal compass, a set of criteria or guidelines for designing the other aspects of our life to be more engaging and fulfilling.

I strongly encourage you to do this work before you move on to the rest of the book. You will need the insights you get from these exercises to get the best from the following chapters.

You will benefit from really taking time to reflect on the exercises and questions in this book. After each chapter, expect your ideas to take time to settle and refine. You will find that as you move into the successive sections of this chapter you will get new insights which will cause you to cycle back and improve your understanding of each of the elements that give you meaning.

In each section I have proposed several exercises to help you uncover your values, passions, strengths and purpose. I encourage you to try out a couple of exercises in each section, if not all of them, to stimulate your thinking. Some initial insights may come quickly – it would be surprising if you had reached adulthood without having some idea of what you value – but most people find it useful to write them down and reflect in depth.

Do not be surprised if this process of refinement continues for several weeks. You are reflecting on some of the deepest elements of your character and your life and it makes sense to give your thoughts the time they need to mature.

1. Values – what do you believe in?

Your values are already there in your life, they are what you believe in and what gives meaning, so they will already have been visible at particularly memorable times throughout your life. The exercises in this section help you capture these, make them explicit and explore them in more detail.

I would like to recognize Steve Chamberlain's excellent book *On Purpose* which Steve took me through in my own coaching sessions. This stimulated a lot of my thinking on values and introduced me to the peaks and troughs exercise below.

ANALYSE YOUR PEAKS AND TROUGHS
Start by building a timeline of the ups and downs of your life so far. Think about the peaks and troughs, the highlights and the worst parts of your life so far. They could be significant life events or anything that gave you a sense of meaning or that you remember particularly clearly.

Start with your earliest formative experiences and continue until you are up to date. Draw a simple curve of the ups and downs showing the peaks and the troughs. For the purposes of focusing on what is unique about your values I recommend you leave out experiences that are likely to be common to many people, such as the day you got married, the birth of a child or the death of a loved one. I would expect these to be particularly meaningful experiences for anyone, but they will not necessarily say anything unique about your values.

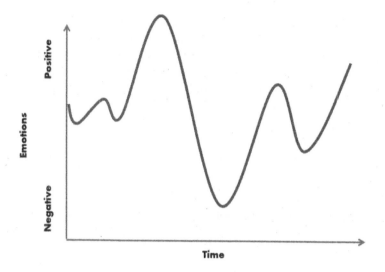

Spend some time thinking about your peaks – your highest positive emotional experiences. For each of these experiences try to recall the experience itself and the emotions that went with it:

• What happened and why?

• Why was it such an important positive experience?

• How did it feel?

• If you could take one factor or piece of learning out of that experience, what would it be?

• What key words describe the experience?

Write down your observations and repeat this for each of your peak positive experiences.

When you have done this, you should have created a list of words that are important to you. You should find patterns emerging, words that come up repeatedly. These words are likely to reflect your values, the things you believe in.

When we have a peak experience, it is usually because we are living or expressing our values. As we move into designing the rest of our lives, we will use this as a template to ask how we can design in more opportunities to feel this way and express these values.

Now repeat the exercise for your low points, the troughs on your curve. Again, try to recall the experience and emotions and capture the learning and write down the words that this suggests. Think about what was missing at this point in your life or what you could have done to avoid this situation or to make it better.

People usually find that their troughs were when they were unable to live according to their values or when they felt compelled to act against the things that they think are profoundly important.

Words that describe my peak experiences	Words that describe my trough experiences

WHAT ARE MY TOP SIX VALUES AND WHAT DO THEY MEAN TO ME? At this point you have produced a lengthy list of words that really resonate for you. Next, look to see if there are any patterns or words that describe various aspects of the same thing. Try to boil them down to around three to six words if you can. Circle words that have resonance or meaning to you and remove any words that you think are not so important.

At this stage you are looking for words that are important to you and **you think always will be**.

You probably have some high-level words on your list, such as 'community', but that could mean quite different things to different people. Use the format below to describe in your own words what these values mean to you and then rank them from 1 to 6 (add more if you feel you must). Prioritizing makes you really think about which of these values are the most important to you.

Ranking	My values	My description of what these words mean to me

ONLINE VALUES SURVEY

There are several online tools that can help you clarify your values. Do not go straight to these, as the previous exercise is much more personal and most online instruments will try to fit you into their existing model.

If you would like an additional perspective, just search for 'online values survey' and you will find several, either free or paid. I found the paid one at www.findyourvalues.com particularly helpful and it includes a report with more information and explanations.

You can use the information from your online report to compare with the peaks and troughs exercise above. You should find a significant overlap.

SOME COMMON VALUES

Here is a list of common values. You can use it to spark ideas. Feel free to add other words. Circle the words that you think most strongly describe you and cross out any that do not. I suggest you do not try this until you have done at least the peaks and troughs exercise so that you are not drawn into just selecting the values you think are good or desirable – choose the ones that really reflect who you are already and what you believe in.

Acceptance	Accessibility	Accomplishment
Accountability	Accuracy	Achievement
Activeness	Adaptability	Advancement
Adventure	Affection	Affluence
Agility	Alertness	Altruism
Amazement	Ambition	Appreciation
Approachability	Artistry	Assertiveness
Attentiveness	Audacity	Authenticity
Authority	Autonomy	Availability
Awareness	Awe	Balance
Beauty	Being the best	Belonging
Benevolence	Bliss	Boldness
Bravery	Brilliance	Buoyancy
Calmness	Camaraderie	Candour
Capability	Carefulness	Caring
Certainty	Challenge	Change

Charity	Charm	Cheerfulness
Citizenship	Clarity	Clear-mindedness
Cleverness	Closeness	Comfort
Commitment	Common sense	Community
Compassion	Competence	Competition
Composure	Concentration	Confidence
Conformity	Connection	Consciousness
Conservation	Contentment	Contributing
Control	Conviction	Conviviality
Coolness	Cooperation	Cordiality
Correctness	Courage	Courtesy
Creativity	Credibility	Curiosity
Daring	Decisiveness	Decorum
Dedication	Delight	Dependability
Determination	Development	Devotion
Dignity	Diligence	Directness
Discipline	Discovery	Discretion
Diversity	Dominance	Drive
Duty	Dynamism	Ease
Economy	Education	Effectiveness
Efficiency	Elegance	Empathy
Empower	Encouragement	Endurance
Enjoyment	Entertainment	Enthusiasm
Entrepreneurial	Environmentalism	Qualité
Equanimity	Ethics	Excellence
Excitement	Expertise	Exploration
Expressiveness	Fairness	Faith
Family	Fearlessness	Feelings
Fidelity	Financial independence	Firmness
Fitness	Flexibility	Focus
Forgiveness	Fortitude	Frankness
Freedom	Friendliness	Frugality
Fun	Generosity	Giving

Goodness	Grace	Gratitude
Gregariousness	Growth	Happiness
Challenging work	Harmony	Health
Helpfulness	Heroism	Holiness
Home	Honesty	Honour
Hopefulness	Hospitality	Humanity
Humility	Humour	Imagination
Impact	Impartiality	Improvement
Independence	Individuality	Inner Harmony
Innovation	Inquisitiveness	Insightfulness
Inspiring	Integrity	Intensity
Intimacy	Introspection	Intuitiveness
Inventiveness	Involvement	Joy
Justice	Kindness	Knowledge
Learning	Liberty	Logic
Longevity	Love	Loyalty
Mindfulness	Modesty	Mysteriousness
Neatness	Nonconformity	Obedience
Openness	Optimism	Order
Organization	Originality	Outdoors
Outrageousness	Patience	Peace
Perfection	Performance	Persistence
Personal Development	Philanthropy	Piety
Playfulness	Poise	Popularity
Popularity	Power	Pragmatism
Precision	Preparedness	Pride
Privacy	Proactivity	Productivity
Proficiency	Professionalism	Prosperity
Prudence	Punctuality	Purity
Purpose	Rationality	Rationality
Realism	Reasonableness	Reciprocity
Recognition	Recreation	Reflection
Relaxation	Reliability	Reputation

Resilience	Resolution	Resolve
Resourcefulness	Respect	Responsibility
Restraint	Results-oriented	Reverence
Rigour	Risk	Sacrifice
Security	Self-control	Selflessness
Self-Reliance	Sensitivity	Sensuality
Serenity	Service	Sexuality
Sharing	Shrewdness	Significance
Silence	Silliness	Simplicity
Sincerity	Skilfulness	Solidarity
Solitude	Sophistication	Speed
Spirit	Spiritualism	Spontaneity
Stability	Status	Stewardship
Strength	Structure	Success
Support	Surprise	Sustainability
Sympathy	Teaching	Teamwork
Temperance	Thankfulness	Thoroughness
Thoughtfulness	Thrift	Tidiness
Timeliness	Tolerance	Toughness
Traditional	Tranquillity	Transcendence
Trustworthiness	Truth	Understanding
Unflappability	Uniqueness	Usefulness
Valour	Variety	Vigour
Virtue	Vitality	Volunteering
Warmth	Watchfulness	Wealth
Welcoming	Wellness	Winning
Wisdom	Wonder	Wonder
Worthiness	Youthfulness	Zeal

WHERE DO YOUR VALUES INTERSECT?

Once you are comfortable with your basic list of values, it can be extremely useful to think through how these values influence each other and what happens when they come into tension.

Put your list of values into both axes and think about what happens when they meet. For example, consider situations where your first value and your second value come into conflict or occur at the same time. How do you resolve this? What happens when your values are in tension?

	Value 1	2	3	4	5	6
Value 1						
2						
3						
4						
5						
6						

For example, one of my values is around 'achievement' and another is 'autonomy'. It was interesting to reflect on how, as my business became more successful, it sometimes meant I needed to do things I did not really enjoy because they were the right things to grow the business. I realized I had fallen into an imbalance by prioritizing achievement too much over autonomy. I was then able to focus on getting a better balance.

The answers to these questions will help uncover what these values really mean to you and how you live your life when they are in tension.

CHALLENGE QUESTIONS
Here are some other questions you can ask yourself that may illustrate aspects of your values. If the answers to these questions are quite different from the values you have produced so far, then you may want to spend more time reflecting on what your values really are.

- What is most important in your life? Beyond your basic human needs, what *must* you have in your life to experience fulfilment?

- What were the life and work experiences where you felt most alive or proud?

- What are the five things you most admire in others?

- When are you at your absolute best?

- What would you like your family and friends to say about you?

- What gives you most energy (or takes your energy away)?

These are deep questions, so be prepared for this to take some time. If it takes a lot of thought and reflection, then you are doing it right.

DESCRIBE YOUR PERFECT DAY

While your values are fresh in your mind, it can be a useful consolidation exercise to spend some time thinking about your perfect day. What would you be doing? Who would you be with? Where would you be? Try to imagine it in as much detail as you can, visualize the events and feel the emotions associated with them.

The likelihood is that this day is one that allows you to express some or all your deepest values. If your perfect day expresses things that are quite different from the values you have produced so far, you might want to go back and consider whether something is missing from your values list.

What would be your perfect day? What values will you be living on that perfect day?

2. Passions – what do you love to do?

The second lens we will look through to find meaning is to focus on what we love to do, our passions.

If you have a real passion in your life, you already know what it is. Passions are all-encompassing, they are things that you could not imagine being absent from your life. If you read the literature on passion, you see stories about people who walked past a piano practice room aged six, heard someone playing and never wanted to do anything else but become a concert pianist for the rest of their lives. This is a beautiful story and you are extremely fortunate if you have something like this in your life. However, many people do not have a single life passion like this. Many have several, often less intense, passions.

When I was searching for my passion, I struggled to find one big thing. When I went back to my values, I realized that as one of them was variety, it would be unlikely that just one thing would fulfil this need. I realized that what I really enjoy is learning new things. I was often criticized for taking up a new hobby, studying it obsessively, buying all the books and equipment and then losing interest. I realized my true passion was learning and once I understood something enough, I was free to move on to the next topic.

This was also an extremely useful excuse for me to be able to justify buying all the equipment for my next interest and countering the objection 'this will all end up in the loft', which is true.

If something is a real passion for you, it has the following charac-teristics:

- You cannot imagine not having it in your life.

- You love to spend time on it and you find time for it.

- It causes you to lose all sense of time.

- It gives you energy and fires your imagination.

- You are prepared to make sacrifices for it.

Do you already know what your passion is?

You may find that reflecting on your values has already given you some ideas about your passion. If it is not immediately obvious what your passions are, do not worry, they may well emerge from some of the exercises below or as we explore your strengths and purpose.

I found that a lot of people, particularly us Brits, feel uncomfortable with the notion of passion. It is a strong word, so I created a scale of positive emotions and engagement.

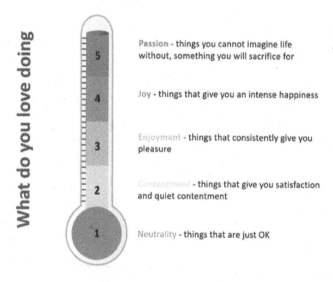

Passion - things you cannot imagine life without, something you will sacrifice for

Joy - things that give you an intense happiness

Enjoyment - things that consistently give you pleasure

Contentment - things that give you satisfaction and quiet contentment

Neutrality - things that are just OK

(vertical label: What do you love doing)

WHAT ACTIVITIES AND EXPERIENCES IN YOUR LIFE AND WORK FALL INTO THESE CATEGORIES?

If you have something that is a 5 on this scale – a real passion – how do you feel when you are doing it? Where did this passion come from? What do you give up to be available to do it? There will be very few of these, but they will be particularly important to you.

Things that cause joy (a 4 on our scale) bring an experience of intense happiness. They are often events of short duration, a time when you laugh aloud with the pleasure of the experience. Moments of joy are often ones we spend with other people (it is quite rare to burst out laughing when you are on your own).

You have a larger number of experiences that cause enjoyment (level 3 on our scale). Moments of enjoyment are usually more sustainable, longer-term sources of happiness rather than peak experiences. Having a lot of enjoyment in your life is a solid basis for a happy life.

Let us not undervalue having a feeling of contentment (level 2). It is OK to be content, particularly if you are a person who does not have strong mood swings either way. Contentment can be a good place to be for everyday things.

Most of us will have some things that are just OK, a neutral experience (level 1). Not all of life is a party. However, it is useful to look at the balance in your life. If you only have 1s then this is a good time to consider building more positive activities into your portfolio so that you can develop a more positive emotional engagement in life and work. We will look at how to do that in future chapters.

Fit your activities and experiences into this scale. Where do you experience these various levels of emotional intensity?

Emotional intensity	Activities and experiences
5 Passion – things you cannot imagine life without, something you will sacrifice for	
4 Joy – things that give you an intense happiness	
3 Enjoyment – things that consistently give you pleasure	
2 Contentment – things that give you satisfaction and quiet contentment	
1 Neutrality – things that are just OK	

OTHER QUESTIONS TO HELP UNCOVER YOUR CURRENT OR POTENTIAL PASSIONS

What do I really love doing?	
When I was young, I always wanted to...	
If I had time to practise more, I would be good at...	
If I had to pick just one interest to spend time on now, it would be...	
What do I want to have more of in my life?	
If money were no object I would...	
What values or principles would I defend to the death?	
What did I used to be passionate about but have lost touch with?	
What do I dream of doing or being?	
Which subject could I talk about for hours?	
What work would feel more like play?	
If I had three months to spend with a world expert in something, when they would teach me all they know, who would it be and what would they teach me?	

WHAT IS YOUR BEST GUESS ON WHAT YOUR PASSIONS ARE AT THIS STAGE?

WHAT COULD DEVELOP INTO MORE OF A PASSION IF YOU GAVE IT MORE TIME AND ATTENTION?

Do any of your activities at levels 3 or 4 have the potential to develop into real passions?

DEEPEN YOUR UNDERSTANDING

Create an enjoyment journal on your phone or in a notebook. Start a page with two columns or sections.

1. What gave me passion, joy or active enjoyment today?

2. What drained my energy or disappointed me about today?

Set an alarm on your phone to review this daily.

You can label the experiences as +2 to +5 on the scale above if they are positive experiences, or -2 to -5 if they are unpleasant experiences.

After a few weeks, go back through your journal and identify the common themes, both positive and negative. This will help you identify your passions and sources of joy and active enjoyment and prompt some ideas about how to spend more time on the things you enjoy and cut out the things you dislike. You will also identify things that drain your energy and make you feel dissatisfied. We can then look at how to design these out of our lives. We will come back to this theme later.

3. Strengths – what are you good at and enjoy doing?

Strengths as I am using the term does not just mean something you are good at; it is also something you positively enjoy doing. As Marcus Buckingham puts it in his book *Now, Discover Your Strengths: How to Develop Your Talents and Those of the People You Manage*, 'A strength is an activity that strengthens you. It draws you in, it makes time fly by while you are doing it, and it makes you feel strong. You, and you alone, can recognize and identify your strengths.'

I want to help you identify and use the strengths, skills, gifts and talents that are meaningful to you and which you are motivated to express.

Strengths are different from skills. You may have learned to do something such as budget management; the strength behind doing it well may be detail orientation or a love of numbers.

We all have inclinations, talents and things that come easy to us (but not necessarily to others). We tend to be best at things that we enjoy doing. If we can build a life around our strengths, we can fulfil our fullest potential.

Leave out any things you are good at but dislike doing. Traditional education often focuses on helping us improve the things we are not good at. Building a portfolio that gives us fulfilment and happiness means building on the things we positively enjoy doing. We want to build on our strengths and spend more time doing the things we are good at and motivated to do, not focus on battling weaknesses and things we dislike.

Use the following exercise to probe more deeply into your strengths.

1. Write down 20 things you are good at and 3 of your main weaknesses.

2. Consider whether your weaknesses are the opposite side of strengths – if you lack attention to detail, this may be sign of being good at taking the broader overview.

3. Think about your natural talents or gifts – the top five things you have been good at since you were young. You may not even remember learning these, they are something you have always done.

4. What strengths (not just skills) have you learned – in your career, profession, function, industry, life? Remember, only include the ones you are good at and enjoy exercising.

5. What have been your greatest successes and peak moments (look back at the work you did on peaks and troughs when looking at your values)? What strengths were you using at these times? What strengths do you exercise when you are at your best?

6. Choose the top six from all the strengths you have identified.

7. If it is one of your 'super strengths':

- it will show up regularly in your successes

- you will naturally use it regularly

- others would notice it in you

- exercising it makes you feel engaged and fulfilled

- time flies when you are exercising it.

WHEN DO I GET TO EXERCISE MY TOP STRENGTHS?

Now take your top six strengths – things you are good at and enjoy. Spend some time thinking about when you get to exercise these strengths in your life and work. These are times when you find strong satisfaction and enjoyment. What could you do to make this happen more often, to give you more opportunities to exercise your strengths? This could be at work or in your hobbies or broader life.

My top strengths	When do I get to exercise these strengths in my life and career?	What changes could I make to realign my life and career more around this strength?

WHAT STRENGTHS DO YOU WANT TO DEVELOP FOR THE NEXT STAGE OF YOUR LIFE?

If you are considering changing role or moving on from full-time work, or you just fancy a change, you may want to apply your strengths in a different context.

Where would you be able to exercise your strengths more often at the next stage of your life? We will come back to this question in our section on the role of work in your portfolio.

You may want to develop some all-new strengths and skills for the next stage of your life, so we will come back to this in the action planning part of the book. You might also want to think about where you could apply your strength in a new context.

GO DEEPER

If you want to spend more time reflecting on your strengths, here are some other exercises you can try.

Ask people who know you well

Sometimes we can be too close to our own strengths to recognize them clearly, particularly the natural strengths which we have always had and sometimes take for granted.

First, ask some people who know you well what they see as your strengths. Then, share your thinking and ask for their comments.

Gardner's Nine Intelligences

Howard Gardner in his book *Frames of Mind: The Theory of Multiple Intelligences* moved away from the idea that there was just one form of generalized intelligence (IQ) and introduced seven (which he later extended to nine) distinct types of intelligence. See if these spark any ideas about your strengths. You may find you have strengths in one or more of these.

Type of intelligence	What are your strengths in these areas?
1. Musical – can make and hear sounds better than others	
2. Logical-Mathematical – recognizing patterns, reasoning and abstract thinking	
3. Interpersonal – can interact with and understand other people well	
4. Bodily-Kinaesthetic – good mind–body coordination and physical skills	
5. Linguistic – good at using words	
6. Intra-personal – the ability to understand yourself	
7. Spatial – able to imagine and visualize things in three dimensions	
8. Naturalistic – sensitive to nature and the environment	
9. Existential – able to consider fundamental questions of life, death and meaning	

Adapted from Howard Gardner, *Frames of Mind: The Theory of Multiple Intelligences*

Online strength finder surveys

Some people find it helpful to complete an online survey to help discover their strengths. If you search for 'online strength-finding surveys', you will find a number are available.

One reputable one is offered by Gallup, the Clifton Strengths Finder. Make sure you choose the version for individuals rather than corporations. There is a charge for doing this.

Other surveys are available, so search for one that you think would be helpful.

USE THIS LIST OF STRENGTHS TO TRIGGER IDEAS

Some people find it helps to use a list of strengths to spark ideas. Circle the ones below that resonate most for you or which may spark other ideas. Feel free to add your own. Be careful not to fall into the trap of just choosing words that you think are desirable. The words you choose should be things you are already good at and enjoy doing.

Ability to execute	Accountability	Accuracy
Action-oriented	Adaptable	Adventurous
Ambitious	Analytical	Appreciative
Artistic	Assertive	Athletic
Authenticity	Big-picture thinking	Bravery
Building relationships	Building trust	Business acumen
Business planning	Calmness	Caring
Celebrator	Challenging	Change
Charming	Client relations	Closing sales
Coding	Collaboration	Collecting
Communication	Community builder	Compassion
Competing	Composing	Computer skills
Confidence	Conflict management	Consensus building
Constructive criticism	Continuous Improvement	Coordination
Cost control	Creating dialogue	Creativity
Critical thinking	Cultural competence	Curiosity
Customer service	Dealing with ambiguity	Dealing with difficult people
Dealmaking	Debating	Decision making

Delegation	Designing	Detail-oriented
Developing people	Digital literacy	Disciplined
Dispute resolution	Drive for achievement	Effective listener
Emotional intelligence	Empathy	Empowering
Energy	Entertaining	Enthusiasm
Entrepreneurship	Ethical	Evidence finder
Experimenting	Exploring	Facilitation
Fairness	Finance	Finding resources
Fixing problems	Fixing things	Flexibility
Focused	Forecasting	Friendliness
Getting things started	Getting to the heart of it	Goal planning
Grateful	Growing things	Handling stress
Healing	Helpful	Humorous
Idea generator	Imagination	Industrious
Influencing	Information technology	Inspirational
Inspiring	Interpersonal skills	Involving others
Judgement	Justice	Kindness
Languages	Leadership	Learning
Listening	Logical	Maintenance
Making change happen	Making new connections	Making things
Management	Marketing	Mathematics
Meeting management	Mentorship	Multi-lingual
Negotiation	Networking	Numbers
Objection handling	Objectivity	Observant
Operating	Optimistic	Organized
Outgoing	Overcoming obstacles	Pathfinder
Performing	Persistent	Perspective
Persuasive	Physical movement	Physical strength
Planning	Practical	Presenting
Problem solving	Process improvement	Product development
Project management	Prototyping	Public relations
Public speaking	Quality control	Questioner
Relationship management	Repairing things	Research

Revenue generation	Risk management	Science
Seeing the big picture	Self-belief	Self-control
Self-direction	Self-improvement	Selling ideas
Social skills	Stakeholder management	Storytelling
Strategic	Strong	Stylish
Systems thinking	Tactful	Taking initiative
Teaching / Training	Team building	Tidying up
Time management	Translating things	Troubleshooting
Trustworthy	Versatile	Visionary
Welcoming	Wisdom	Writing

CONSOLIDATION

Use this space or a separate piece of paper to bring together the work you have done so far in this section around values, passions and strengths – these are all important elements of what gives meaning to you. Having them at the forefront of your mind will help you in the next step, which is to define your purpose.

My values

My values	How well are they expressed in my life?	How can I express them more?

My passions

My passions	How well are they expressed in my life?	How can I spend more of my time on them?

My strengths

My strengths	How do I exercise these strengths in my life today?	How can I exercise them more?

BRINGING IT TOGETHER IN A PURPOSE STATEMENT

Now we have looked at what gives meaning to us from several different angles, we can start to think about what the overall purpose to our lives is. Your purpose describes your main motivating aims and goals, why you get up in the morning. For some people, the thought of life purpose can be too big a question. A simpler way of thinking about it is, 'How should I spend my time in ways that are important to me?'

According to research by McKinsey, about 85 per cent of people feel that they have a purpose, but only 65 per cent believe they can articulate it.

If you are clear about your purpose, it can help guide your decisions, give direction and create meaning. If you cannot write it down, it is hard to use it as a guide.

While some people may have a singular purpose that engages them for the whole of their lives, it is often easier to think about the purpose for your next 5–10 years. The purpose you set yourself in your 30s may be quite different from the one you set yourself in your 60s. Because of this, you may choose to revisit your purpose from time to time as you update your life plan.

You may also find you have multiple purposes in different areas of your life, so do not obsess about finding one single statement that sums up everything you are trying to achieve. Your values, passions and strengths will change much more slowly, but what you apply them to do will naturally change over time.

I found that a useful format for writing a purpose statement answers the questions 'what' and 'why'. What will I do and why will I do it?

My purpose is to . . . .

in order to . . . .

As an example of bringing these elements together, I will share my own findings from these exercises. Yours of course will be different (each of us has a unique set), but I hope this will help show how you can integrate the outputs from the previous exercises into your purpose statement.

My values were:

- multigenerational family success and happiness

- continuing to achieve and learn

- enjoying a variety of experiences

- retaining autonomy and freedom

- living in good health

- enjoying the moment

- building new community and relationships.

  My strengths were:

- seeing opportunities in uncertainty

- creating better ways to do things

- communicating them to others.

My passion is learning new things.

My purpose draws on the most important elements of each of these: to explore new learning, experiences and relationships in order to support my own wellbeing and that of my family.

Have a try at creating your own purpose statement using this format.

My purpose is to . . . .

in order to . . . .

By now you should have an improved understanding of your values, passions, strengths and purpose. Set aside some time to reflect on this and discuss it with people who know you well. Does it resonate with them? Is there something missing?

It helps to write these down and post them somewhere visible to keep them at the forefront of your mind.

- Purpose gives direction – it is an inner compass to follow in deciding how you want to spend your time.

- Your values keep you on the path – if you act in a way that is consistent with your values, you will find your activities meaningful.

- Your passions give you energy – allocate more of your time to the things that give you joy and enjoyment and less to the things that do not.

- Your strengths are the things you are good at and enjoy doing – look for opportunities to exercise them more often and apply them in all areas of your life.

As we move into the next stages of the book, we will keep coming back to these insights in designing our work, leisure and other activities in a way that brings meaning, fulfilment and enjoyment.

You will find that your understanding of your values, passions, strengths and purpose evolves as you work through the book and you may develop additional insights. I suggest capturing your initial ideas but coming back to them after you finish the book, or in a few weeks' time, to see if your thinking has developed. It often takes some time and some reflection to produce the finished versions.

CHAPTER 4

Building Your Own Engagement at Work

* * *

Many of us spend around 40 per cent of our waking lives at work for over 40 years, which is more than 80,000 hours of our lives. Some get paid, others do some form of unpaid work such as caring or volunteering. How we spend that time and how we feel about it has a major impact on the quality of our lives.

According to the Gallup State of the Global Workplace 2022 Report, only 20 per cent of people are positively engaged at work, 60 per cent are emotionally detached and 20 per cent are miserable, so most people have a significant block of what they feel is poor-quality time in their working lives.

While our employers and leaders have a role in improving our experience of work, as individuals this is too big a problem for us to leave it to others to solve. How we spend our time is the quality of our life. It is in our interests to become more engaged at work if we want a fulfilling and happy life.

Even those of us who are fully engaged at work are seeing the nature of work changing. The chances are that most of us will be working for longer and making the transition between distinct types of work, different technologies and varying roles more often than in the past.

As people become healthier, retirement ages are increasing and over half of people over retirement age still expect to be involved in work of some kind, either through choice or because they need the income – 18 per cent expect to be working full time.

Technological change means that people earlier in their working lives are likely to be retraining and taking on quite different roles more than once in their career. The growth of freelancing and the gig economy and the decline of the idea of a job for life mean that work will become more varied and more transient.

Those who do not work in the sense of paid employment can use the principles in this chapter to think about getting maximum meaning from how they perform their hobbies, interests, caring responsibilities or other forms of activity.

Given the central part that work plays in our lives, if we are not happy and fulfilled in our work, then it is impossible to have an overall fulfilled and happy life. This chapter will show you how to create more engagement and happiness for yourself at work.

The paradox of work – mindset matters

Work is a paradox, it provides some of our most intense and satisfying moments, it can generate a feeling of accomplishment, pride and identity. At its best we get a lot out of work, and usually we get paid as well.

But sometimes work can be too demanding, it can take up time you would rather spend on other goals and it can be something you feel you have to do rather than something you want to do. There can be factors in the job itself, such as job dissatisfaction, work overload, lack of challenge or problems with your colleagues or boss. In these circumstances work can feel like a chore.

The three main reasons people resent work are:

1. They feel their job is pointless and does no good to anyone.

2. The work itself is boring and routine or it provides no variety or challenge.

3. The work is stressful or feels undervalued, especially if you do not have a good relationship with your supervisor or colleagues.

And yet most of us need to work to look after our families and have a decent life. How we experience and feel about work is essential to being engaged and happy for 40 per cent of our waking life.

In previous generations, people worked long hours and often in tough conditions. Leisure was seen as the antidote. But fewer people nowadays have hard physical roles and knowledge workers are not physically worn out by their 60s; some are just coming into their prime. As we will see in Chapter 7, just having more leisure is not enough for a happy and fulfilling life – it turns out to be more difficult to use our leisure time more positively than we expect.

At the time of writing there was a, hopefully brief, trend on the subject of 'quiet quitting', where people quietly do the minimum to get by in their work to focus on other things. That is a terrible idea, both for career success and for life happiness. Wouldn't it be better to find a way to positively enjoy your work?

There are few areas of life where we get more out of an experience by putting less effort in and work is not one of them. In this chapter, I will introduce techniques you can use to re-engineer whatever type of work you choose and change your attitudes towards it to make it more fulfilling.

Finding flow

Mihaly Csikszentmihalyi, a Hungarian psychologist and author of *Finding Flow: The Psychology of Engagement with Everyday Life*, monitored in detail what people spent their time doing and how they were feeling about it. He identified the concept of 'flow', a state that happened when someone was dealing with a higher-than-average level of challenge and exercising a higher-than-average level of skill. The more regularly a person was in this state of flow, the more likely they were to report a high quality of experience. They described themselves as feeling active, creative, concentrated, motivated and strong.

You know when you are in flow because time passes quickly, you are focused and productive. People experiencing a below-average number of challenges and using a below-average number of skills describe themselves as feeling dull, dissatisfied, passive, weak and apathetic.

Overall, people reported being in flow on average about 33 per cent of the time. However, this was made up of being in flow for 54 per cent of their time at work, and only 18 per cent during leisure.

Managers experience flow more often than office workers, who in turn experience flow more often than blue-collar workers, so the kind of work we do is important.

Csikszentmihalyi also asked people at regular points during the day whether they would rather be doing something different. When working, even if people were experiencing flow, they said they would rather be doing something else. When during leisure time, even if it was not particularly interesting, they were content to keep doing it.

When adolescents are doing something labelled as work, they say it is important for their future, requires high concentration and induces high self-esteem. Yet they are less happy and motivated than average. When they are doing something they label as play, they see it as having low importance, requiring little concentration, but they are happy and motivated.

Redesigning your work life for meaning and engagement

As we saw, according to Gallup, only 20 per cent of people are positively engaged at work. Usually, we blame leaders for not creating the right environment for their people. In this book, however, we are all about taking personal responsibility for our lives, so we are going to focus on what **we** can do to create our own engagement.

It is great if our leaders create an environment where we can do this effortlessly, but that is not always the case. You cannot control your company or your boss, but you can control your attitude and how you approach your work. Why not step up and create the engagement you deserve in your life?

The quality of your life is how you spend your hours. Can you afford to be disengaged? If your work is making you actively miserable, you should make a change.

If you allow your work to be boring and tedious then you are choosing to live a large part of your life in this state – this is your problem, you cannot wait for someone else to fix your life. It will be no consolation to be able to blame your boss for 40 wasted years after you retire.

Companies redesign jobs continuously to meet their needs, this is called job design. Job reengineering (or job crafting) is where individuals redesign their own jobs to make them more engaging and fulfilling. Companies like Google and Virgin have experimented with this approach, but in most cases you can simply start doing this yourself.

This is about exercising choice and taking ownership for your job. Do not just passively accept what happens at work or wait until someone else brings change, look for alternative ways to do things yourself. Even if no one else notices, you will have a more satisfying job – remember, you are doing this for yourself, not for someone else.

If there are major changes needed, you may need to negotiate them with your manager. In many cases, however, you can start to make changes yourself without them even noticing. Nevertheless, if you do need to negotiate these changes, you can show your manager how this will make you more effective and tell them that academic studies have linked job crafting to better performance, higher intrinsic motivation and improved employee engagement.

If you want to systematically reengineer your current role, this means working on four key areas:

1. Tasks – do more of the things you enjoy, minimize the things you do not, build new skills and challenges.

2. Relationships – improve your relationships and interactions with others.

3. Attitude – how can I make what I do more valuable and meaningful to me? How can I continue to learn and reframe my experience of work?

4. Location – how can I work from a location that motivates me or removes things that I am dissatisfied with?

Whatever types of work you choose as part of your portfolio, the principles below can help you design it for more engagement and happiness.

You can start by working on these yourself. This section also forms an excellent team discussion where you may be able to trade responsibilities with other people so that you each get more of what you enjoy.

REDESIGNING THE TASKS
This involves changing the tasks themselves or the sequence and flow of the tasks you perform in your work.

• Take each step of your job – can you do each of them better or faster?

• How can you make your contribution more valuable to others and meaningful to you?

- How can you take on new tasks, streamline your existing tasks or processes, or spend more time exercising your strengths in your current role?

- As you look at the flow of your work, are there any bottlenecks, places or stages where things get held up or routinely go wrong? How can you design these out of the process?

- How can you change the balance of your time to spend more time on the things you enjoy and less time on the things you dislike?

- Where can you volunteer to get involved in new projects or activities that move you towards areas you are interested in and help you build new skills?

- How can you adjust the balance of skills and challenge to achieve more flow?

Seek flow – make it a game

In his writing about flow, Csikszentmihalyi often refers to 'being in the zone', where people are challenged to exercise their skills, time passes quickly and we report high levels of energy and satisfaction. Achieving flow is about having stretching goals and about building your skills to meet and achieve them.

While thinking about this chapter, I saw a wonderful video of someone cleaning the windows of a coffee shop two-handed to music. They had turned their work into an art form and at the end of it they received a round of applause from the people in the shop. They had taken what is not the most interesting job in the world and turned it into an artistic performance; they genuinely looked as though they were enjoying the experience.

Instead of waiting for our leaders to create an environment where we are engaged, shouldn't we take individual responsibility for our own engagement, seek out more challenging goals and work on developing our skills? The more energy and passion we invest in our jobs, the more we get back in return – maybe not always financially but certainly in terms of enjoyment and meaning.

If you work to be the best at your job and you do not feel you get the recognition you deserve, then at least you have a great story to tell at your next job interview. Or you could go back to being emotionally detached for 40 per cent of your life – it is your life, so you get to choose, but do not blame someone else if you make that choice.

Achieving flow is about using your skills to address challenges. If we get stuck in a place where our challenges are not enough to stretch our skills, or where our skills are not developing because our challenges are too easy, then we become bored.

What is the balance for you right now?

Where specifically do you feel that the challenges you face exceed your skills to deal with them?	Where specifically do you feel that the skills you already have exceed the challenges you normally face?

Here is a straightforward way to improve the probability of you achieving flow depending on your answers above:

- For the areas where you feel that the challenges you face exceed your skills to deal with them – build your skills.

- For the areas where you feel that the skills you already have exceed the challenges you normally face – seek out bigger challenges.

It may seem too simple, but what we are doing is initiating a growth spiral of taking on new challenges and developing new skills.

Some people are concerned that if they take on more challenges it will lead to negative experiences. They can feel anxious when they perceive that the challenges they face exceed the skills they have. Where you feel there is an existing imbalance, focus on your skills first. Then seek out progressively higher levels of challenge.

Csikszentmihalyi found that the flow state was characterized by:

- exercising above-average skills

- working on above-average challenges

- getting more feedback on progress and success

- some structure or rules so you know when you win.

This is why high-level sports and games are so popular: they are designed to create a state of flow.

Some of my most intense and sustained experiences of flow were in my past hobby as an amateur rally driver. As I developed more skills, I sought out more challenging events, which then made new gaps in my skills visible. When you are driving fast on a slippery surface through a forest you need to be in the zone at all times. It was a constant 'arms race' between skill and challenge, and I could measure my progress on the event leader boards.

Build on your strengths

At school, and often at work, we are encouraged to work on our weaknesses. If only we could improve in areas where we are currently weak, surely we could be more well rounded and productive? However, this does not necessarily lead to superior performance, and there is no chance you will build a fulfilled and enjoyable portfolio of activities based on doing things you do not enjoy or must force yourself to do.

You may even have worked out how to do some of the things you dislike well. But doing more of this is unlikely to help. For our purposes, I define strengths as something we are good at **and** we enjoy.

You should already have identified your strengths through the exercises in Chapter 3. If you want to create an even more engaging job or work experience, focus on building in or finding even more opportunities to exercise your strengths.

What are my strengths?	What type of work would give me most opportunity to exercise my strengths?	How can I find more opportunities to exercise my strengths in my current job?

It can be hard to exercise all your strengths in just one job. If you have key strengths that you cannot exercise in your current work, you may find opportunities to do this in your leisure, in your hobbies (see Chapter 7) or in some other work sideline.

Which of my strengths do I *not* get to exercise at work?	What other work side lines, hobbies or activities could I try to exercise my unused strengths?

ELIMINATE, STREAMLINE, AUTOMATE OR OUTSOURCE THE PARTS OF THE JOB YOU DO NOT ENJOY

We can increase the average enjoyment in our job by cutting out the things we enjoy the least. Try these things, in this order:

1. What tasks can you **eliminate** – what would happen if you just stopped doing these things? When I started a new job early in my career I would usually begin with external reporting. I would just quietly stop producing standard reports and information and see if anyone noticed – they hardly ever did. If you want to be more cautious, identify what you see as being the lowest-value work you produce and check in with key stakeholders whether they really require this work.

2. Can the work be **streamlined** or simplified to reduce the amount of work or speed up its delivery? Produce a flow chart of how you do the work and look for opportunities to take out, combine or simplify stages. Look for anything that slows down completion of the work and try to engineer it to be more effective. If you have routine tasks that sap your energy, it can be good practice to cluster a number of these together on one afternoon per week and blitz through them, rather than having a few to do every day.

   In my reporting example, if I could not just stop doing it, I would look at where I was duplicating information to different people and see if the same report could be used for several requests. I would look for simpler ways to give people the information they needed. When I asked people what information they really used, it would often be only a small subset of what they usually received.

   As a manager I took over a large manufacturing facility and after the first month spent four long hours going through my new budgets and accounts with an accountant to understand what they were telling me. By the end of four hours, I had identified that there were only really two things that mattered: scrap and labour utilization. They represented 95 per cent of my costs and the other 45 pages of financial information were just a distraction from focusing on those two things. I then asked for just these two numbers on one piece of paper so that I was not distracted by all the other irrelevant stuff.

3. What tasks can you **automate**? Is there work you can move into an online system? Do your office tools such as Excel, Word and Outlook have functions that could make work easier? If this is not within your power to act upon, can you make a case for greater automation to support your role? As artificial intelligence becomes more embedded in office tools, you should expect that more of your routine work will be automated. Instead of seeing this as a threat, embrace it and use it to make your work more interesting.

4. What can you **outsource**? Is there work you can get someone else to do? Another person might see the work as a development opportunity – maybe a colleague, subordinate or external supplier can pick it up? As a manager, I realized that some of the things I did not enjoy doing could be development opportunities for others who wanted to learn something new or could exercise their strengths that I did not share. From my budget example above, while I focused on my top two factors of scrap and labour, I gave the rest of the financial report to a graduate trainee to monitor and work on as their first experience in managing a budget.

5. Can you change your **mindset** about the work? By looking at the meaning of our work, the impact on our customers and colleagues, or the world in general, we can sometimes change the way we think about our work and reframe our tasks in a way that makes them more engaging.

Work can bring meaning at three levels:

- as a job – it pays the bills and allows us to satisfy our basic needs

- as a career – it gives us a development path, a sense of progression and, often, social esteem

- as a calling or vocation – where we are inspired by the work itself and its meaning.

As an exercise, pick a task from your calendar such as attending a meeting, making a presentation or working on a document. Think about how you would approach this if it were just a job, then how you would approach it if it were important to your career, and finally how you would approach it if it were your true vocation or calling in life. How did your emotions change as you approached the task from different perspectives? Try doing this with other tasks, or even an entire day. What would your job be like if you were operating at each of these three levels?

Do be realistic – even the best jobs have some mundane elements. You are unlikely to be able to eliminate these completely, but most of us do have the opportunity to change the balance to make our job overall more meaningful and enjoyable. Set yourself the target of replacing the least interesting two hours of your week with two hours spent on work you enjoy. If that works, go for two more.

IMPROVING YOUR RELATIONSHIPS AT WORK

The quality of your relationships at work has an enormous impact on how much you enjoy your time there. In this area consider:

- Who do I want to spend time with?

- How can I create more fulfilling relationships at work, including repairing poor relationships or changing my work so I avoid them?

- How can I build my network?

- How can I change who I socialize with and where?

- Could I become a coach or mentor to share my skills and learn new ones myself?

- How can I show a genuine interest in colleagues?

- Where can I find more diverse relationships to expose me to different perspectives and ideas?

- How can I build a relationship with the people who use the outputs or results of my work?

You will get some more ideas on building and improving relationships from Chapter 6.

CHANGING YOUR MINDSET OR ATTITUDE TO YOUR WORK
Sometimes we cannot change the world, but we can change how we feel about it. This area includes looking for more meaning in your work and focusing on why your job is significant to you, your organization, customers and colleagues.

- Where can I find more meaning by living my values, exercising my strengths, pursuing my passions or finding my purpose more at work?

- Where can I engage more with customers (internal or external) to bring more value to my work and better understand how the outputs of what I do have an impact on others?

- Where can I continue to learn and develop?

- Where does work have a positive impact on my life?

- Where can I reframe some of my challenges in my current job as opportunities to develop and grow?

We spent a lot of time in Chapter 3 looking at what brings meaning to our lives: our values, passions, strengths and purpose. If we can connect these elements to the work we do, we will find more meaning and engagement in whatever activity we choose.

- Where does your work align with your values and what you believe in? Many people in healthcare, for example, are motivated by the connection between what they do and the wellbeing of their patients.

- How can you pursue your passion at work? If you have a passion for creativity or design, could you exercise more of this as part of your job?

- How does your work help you achieve your purpose? As a minimum it is helping you to fund the other things in your life, but how else can work contribute to you achieving the purpose you developed for yourself in Chapter 3?

- Can you find value and connect yourself to the purpose of the
  organization you work with? There is an apocryphal story about
  President John F. Kennedy visiting NASA in 1962. He asked a
  janitor what he did for NASA and the janitor replied, 'I'm helping
  put a man on the moon.' That sounds more meaningful than
  mopping the floor.

REFRAMING YOUR EXPERIENCE OF WORK

Our framing of a situation and the expectations coming from this
can become self-fulfilling prophecies. If we see something as negative,
we tend to notice even more of the negatives and filter out the positives.

When we reframe something, we choose to look at it in a different
way. Because our beliefs automatically generate their own supporting
evidence, we can start to change our experience of work and life by
trying out new perspectives.

Here are some reframes you could try about your job:

- Reframing is particularly powerful when it relates to one of your
  values, so if one of your values is family or achievement, how can
  you link these to your work experience and find more meaning?
  Try reframing your work to be more connected to the values you
  have identified as important to you.

- Switch the focus. Instead of asking 'Why is my work not
  engaging?', ask yourself, 'Why am I not engaging myself at work?'

- Imagine a future situation or a future self where your problem is
  already solved. If you find your job boring, imagine what would
  be different if your job were mostly fun.

- Spend time regularly appreciating the things that are already
  going well in your job.

- Consider where any negative beliefs about work came from. Have
  these beliefs helped you in life? Would you choose these beliefs
  again if you revisited what caused them? If you could choose to
  believe something else, what would it be?

Wharton School professor Adam Grant has shown that where people see their work as a form of giving, they tend to consider their jobs as more meaningful. You can encourage this by becoming more connected with the people who are the beneficiaries of your work. For example, Grant found that fundraisers in a university call centre spent 142 per cent more time on the phone and raised 171 per cent more cash once they had met a student who was a beneficiary of the scheme. Focus on your internal and external customers and how what you do has an impact on them.

Most people work to support their families, to enjoy vacations or hobbies, or to be able to afford the extras in life. If we focus on the impact on our families and our lifestyle, then we may see more meaning in our work. Reframing our work as valuable to others, particularly our loved ones, can help make it feel more meaningful.

Pursue intrinsic rewards

Most people work for a combination of intrinsic and extrinsic motivational reasons.

- Extrinsic rewards are financial or other rewards that are usually given to us and controlled by other people. They often bring a limited and short-term emotional boost (remember how that last pay rise motivated you just for a few days and then became the norm?).

- Intrinsic rewards are the psychological rewards we get from inside ourselves for doing meaningful work and doing it well. They depend on our own effort and values and tend to create a longer-lasting positive emotional reaction.

Intrinsic rewards are the more powerful motivators and are more within your control. The intrinsic rewards of work are highest in individualized professions where you are free to choose goals and set the difficulty of the task yourself, such as with creative people, entrepreneurs and senior scientists. For many of these people, their life is much more integrated; work is play and play is work.

As you design your portfolio of work, choose things where your motivation comes from within rather than where it depends on decisions or material incentives from other people. You can do this by connecting your work to your purpose and by doing your work to the best of your ability.

Ideally, we choose work where the reward comes from doing the work itself in the moment.

CHANGE THE LOCATION WHERE YOU WORK

One of the few positives from the COVID-19 pandemic was a huge increase in flexibility in work location. Many organizations now offer either fully remote or hybrid working (where people spend part of their time in the office and do part of the work at home). In many countries, employees now have the right to request flexible working and we can expect the drive towards flexibility to continue into new job sectors and with developments like the four-day working week.

Having more flexibility on location can reduce some of the dissatisfiers about work, such as long commute times, and bring new opportunities to improve our work experience. This gives many of us new opportunities to consider:

- Where do I want to work from?

- What pattern of work would allow me to find the right balance of work and other interests?

- Can remote or hybrid working enable me to exercise more autonomy in my work?

As you work to reengineer your tasks, relationships, mindset and location, why not put more of yourself into it, go the extra mile, take on more responsibility and learn new skills? As in most areas of life, the more energy and effort you put into something, the more you get back in return.

BE OPEN TO WORK–LIFE IMBALANCE

When people talk about work–life balance, it is usually in the context of having too much work and not enough life left over. I cannot remember any participant on one of our training programmes over the years who complained about having too much life. However, people who are highly engaged at work and do what they most enjoy tend to blur the boundaries between work and life.

Artists, performers and other creative people often continue their careers into advanced age. Do you think Einstein stopped thinking at 5 pm or Serena Williams made sure to spend only eight hours a day on tennis? Why do the Rolling Stones keep touring?

In finding the right work–life balance, I have found it useful to distinguish between two different concepts:

- work–life integration – how much overlap is there between work time and non-work time?

- work–life balance – is the total time allocated to work and non-work activities OK for you?

WORK–LIFE INTEGRATION

Some people choose to separate roles and prefer a clear dividing line between life and work. This prevents blurring and keeps the roles distinct. If boundaries are clear, they are easier to enforce, but you may lose the benefits of flexibility. A clear separation is more helpful when your home and work roles are quite different and the transition between them is difficult to manage.

Others see benefits in more integration. We all appreciated the ability during the COVID-19 lockdowns to take time during the normal working day to meet personal and family commitments. If we spent a couple of hours on this during the day, we may have needed to spend some time working in the evening to catch up. That seems fair to me.

It is easier to work this way when your work and home roles are more similar (transitions are easier) and you have more control over your working pattern.

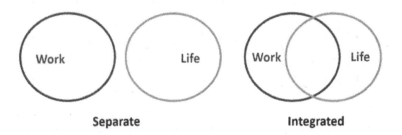

Some people prefer this type of working when work time and family time are intermingled. As we have seen above, this does lead to more blurring of the boundaries, but this may be OK for you.

Benefits of work–life separation	Benefits of work–life integration
• Prevents blurring • Prevents role conflict • Boundaries are easier to enforce	• Gives more flexibility to shift work hours around • Helps us work around other life commitments
• Easier when work and home roles are quite different • More necessary when your job requires a lot of coordination with others	• Easier when home and work roles are more similar • Easier when you can schedule your own working time

I work in a business where other family members are actively involved. We often find business discussions sit naturally alongside family events and we are happy with that as we are all engaged with the success of the business. However, we also make sure that we are available to focus on family-only issues, otherwise business conversations can become all-consuming and boring for those who are not so directly involved.

Each of us may accept a different balance of work and home time, depending on the stage of our career, our personal circumstances and our personality.

WORK–LIFE BALANCE

The key questions with work–life balance are 'How can I be more effective in the time I have available?' and 'How can I say no when the workload becomes too much?'.

I am not talking here about emergencies or exceptional circumstances. Most people are prepared to put in extra hours if the situation is critical. The problem is if long hours become our normal working routine.

• What is your work–life balance/integration like right now? Does it work for you?

- What is your target? What balance would you like to achieve?

- What specifically stops you from getting there?

Be warned, the more you create a work life that is engaging and fulfilling, the harder it will be to maintain your boundaries – and it is perfectly OK to find you do not even want to.

FUTURE PROOF YOUR SKILLS

As artificial intelligence and automation become a larger part of the working environment, some jobs will be replaced by technology and far more will involve working more closely with or being augmented by technology.

Some researchers believe that even 25 per cent of a CEO's job will be automated in future. Consultants PricewaterhouseCoopers estimate that artificial intelligence will create more jobs than it destroys, just like previous waves of technology – but they will be different jobs.

Skills and jobs that rely on following a process, performing a routine manual task or implementing a rule are likely to be most impacted first. If you are coming towards the end of your career, you may not see much of this at work, but you should expect a continuing need to upskill yourself to use the technology that is becoming increasingly embedded in every aspect of life – you will see more on this in Chapter 8. If you are earlier in your career, you should be thinking about future proofing your skills for these developments over the next 10 to 20 years. Pay particular attention to building your skills to work with AI support.

The skills that are likely to be at a premium in an age of increasing automation are the deeply human skills, what used to be called the 'soft skills' – creativity and the ability to communicate, collaborate, influence, lead and engage with other people. Luckily, these are the skills you tend to develop more of as you age.

CONSIDER WHAT YOU ARE PREPARED TO SACRIFICE TO SPEND MORE OF YOUR LIFE ON THE WORK YOU ENJOY

Some people see work as unavoidable just to fund leisure in the future, or eventual retirement. As Randy Komisar, co-founder of Claris, observes in his book *The Monk and the Riddle: The Education of a Silicon Valley Entrepreneur*:

*The most dangerous bet of all is the risk of spending your life
not doing what you want on the bet you can buy yourself the
freedom to do it later.*

It is a risk to put off all the good things until some indeterminate point
in the future.

Part of this is thinking about what you would be prepared to sacrifice in return for a better current life and work experience:

- If you decide to spend less energy on your main job to be
available to develop a side hustle or outside interest, your existing
career could falter as you pay it less attention.

- If you decide to start your own business, there is a chance you
will earn less, particularly at the beginning.

- If you decide to change companies in search of a better role, you
may find it did not really work out.

I hope this chapter will increase the probability of you making a good
decision, but every choice we make has consequences. It is good to be
clear at this point.

- What are you prepared to risk to improve the quality of your
working life?

- What are you not prepared to risk?

HOW CAN LEADERS AND ORGANIZATIONS ENCOURAGE ENGAGEMENT?

I wrote this book for individuals trying to improve their own engagement at work, but engagement is also a key challenge for leaders and
their organizations. Engaged people are more productive, more innova-
tive and provide better customer outcomes. They have lower levels of
absence and report better wellbeing.

Many leading organizations put tremendous effort and investment
into annual employee engagement surveys and activities to help improve
engagement at work. According to the Future Market Insights employee
engagement market outlook survey 2022, organizations were expected
to spend $1.6 billion globally on 'engagement solutions', much of which

would be spent on software platforms to survey and track engagement. This generates a lot of data and high expectations that something will change as a result.

Unfortunately, the current approach has made slow progress on increasing engagement and still only 20 per cent of people say they are highly engaged at work. This can put leaders and Human Resources departments under pressure to 'own' engagement for their people and work to improve their survey scores. While creating an environment where people can be engaged is an important task for leaders, I believe that only individuals can fully create their own engagement at work, and you do not get that from a software platform.

In our corporate work I run workshops and webinars to help people to find their purpose at work and apply the above principles of engagement to redesigning their jobs. Building engagement is a win-win for both organizations and individuals, bringing improved performance and wellbeing.

If you lead people and would like to take them through the process of discovering their purpose and engagement at work, please contact us at www.yourportfoliolife.com.

CHAPTER 5

Designing Your Portfolio Career

● ● ●

You can apply the principles in the previous chapter to any kind of work or activity you decide to do. Now that we have established the principles for choosing meaningful work and engineering it to be more enjoyable, we can think about what types of work are likely to bring us most fulfilment and happiness.

Building a portfolio career

The idea of having a portfolio career was first popularized by Charles Handy in his 1994 book *The Empty Raincoat*. It involves combining a variety of forms of work and sources of income rather than just relying on a single job. It was described more recently by Helen Tupper and Sarah Ellis as having a 'squiggly career'.

The idea is that a linear career of joining a single employer and following a simple hierarchical career ladder for the whole of your working life is outdated. People are starting to move more frequently and more discontinuously into different roles, industries, locations and careers.

- If you are early in your working career, you will need to retrain quite significantly at several points in your work life.

- If you are in the middle of your career, you might find you want more variety, a job or career change, or to try out a side hustle or your own business.

- You may want to prioritize other elements of your life and fit work around that.

- If you are coming towards the end of your traditional working career, you may find that different forms of work come into your portfolio through part-time or self-employed paid work or volunteering.

A portfolio career brings the promise of flexibility and freedom, but it means we need to exercise an informed choice about which forms of work to build into our portfolio.

I have built on this idea of a portfolio career by adding the perspective that it is unlikely we will be able to exercise all our strengths, pursue our passions, live our values and advance our purpose all in one place. We need a variety of work and leisure activities to enable us to be fully engaged and fulfilled.

It can be hard to design a portfolio career unless you are clear about your objectives. In a traditional linear career, you may have joined a company as a human resources trainee with the objective of eventually becoming a human resources director. The pathway and skill development you needed would be clear. It would also be defined around the organization's needs, not yours.

It is up to you to choose your career goals. In this chapter we will look at ways to select types of work that will bring fulfilment and happiness. If you are lucky this may come from just one job; more often it comes from a portfolio of activities.

You may have other ideas. At some point in your life, you might consciously choose to maximize your income or career, even if that comes at a price. I took a job that involved moving my very young family to another country and then travelling to an average of three countries a week for years. It was a tough time, particularly for my wife, and I regret spending that time away from them, but it allowed me to build the skills I needed to start my own business, which then allowed us as a family more autonomy, freedom and flexibility for the next 30 years.

You might choose to follow your passion, irrespective of how much it pays. You might choose work that gives you enormous fulfilment in the moment, even if it does not seem to lead you anywhere. It is fundamentally your choice.

I am a keen scuba diver and regularly meet people who spend their lives following the dive season as instructors and guides around the world. There are others who teach diving in the summer and spend the winter on the ski circuit. Most of them seem to be happy.

If you are more motivated to have a traditional career and a higher level of financial stability, these kinds of roles are unlikely to be more than a passing interest or a holiday fantasy.

Your portfolio career will be based on a direction rather than a destination. If you know that you want to do more of a certain type of work or spend more time on certain types of activities, this may define the next steps in your portfolio career. Happiness and fulfilment are rarely achieved through reaching a destination, they come from enjoying the journey.

You will probably not have a 40-year plan, but you should be thinking about the next 5 to 10 years and the steps within this period that will move you in the direction you want.

In a time of high levels of change it can be impossible to define the endpoint of a career, new opportunities may arise and other avenues may become blocked. A successful portfolio career is not defined by anyone else, so I cannot hand you a guaranteed path to success. However, I can help you develop some criteria and guide rails for choosing the kind of work and the direction you are likely to enjoy. If you enjoy the work, it is more likely you will be good at it.

Pursuing a portfolio career certainly involves lifelong learning and developing new capabilities that open fresh opportunities or keep you up to date with developments. You will get lots more ideas on this in Chapter 8.

DO YOU NEED YOUR WORK TO BE PAID?

In an ideal world we would all do the work we loved without concern for whether it paid the bills. If you are in that position, then celebrate and be happy. For most of us who still need to work, our need for income does impose a constraint. The more money we spend, the more the constraint.

The philosopher Henry David Thoreau observed, 'The price of anything is the amount of life you exchange for it.' At some points in your life, you may choose to prioritize income over free time, at others you may have more freedom to spend your time as you please.

As you work through this chapter, keep in mind how much you need the work part of your life to generate income. If you are considering a discretionary or particularly an indulgent purchase it is an interesting exercise to calculate the number of hours you need to work to buy that latest mobile phone, handbag or car (do not forget to allow for the tax you paid already before the money arrived in your bank account). Is it worth the time you sacrifice from other things?

YOUR CURRENT WORK AUDIT

Let us begin designing our portfolio career by looking at our starting position. How do you feel about the work you do now (however you define work)?

What do you like about your current work?	What do you dislike?

If you want to do this in more detail, keep an activity diary over the next few weeks. Make a note of the work you have been involved with and how meaningful, enjoyable and challenging that work felt at the time. It is best to do this in the moment as it is hard to recall in detail a long time afterwards. Ideally make a note after each piece of work you complete, or alternatively set an hourly alarm on your phone reminding you to record in the format below.

Activity: what work were you doing?	How meaningful was it to you?	How enjoyable was it?	How challenging was it?

As you move into redesigning your work life you can use this information to focus more of your time on the things that are meaningful and enjoyable and look for ways to reduce the time you spend on other things.

I explained in Chapter 4 how building in more challenge is an important part of creating engaging work and achieving flow, so actively build in more of the work that triggers a flow state into your day.

FINDING WORK THAT HAS MEANING FOR YOU

Let us connect back to the work we did on meaning in Chapter 3 and apply what you learned about your passions, values, strengths and purpose to selecting the kind of work that will have most meaning to you. In each area we will ask you to think about what kind of work would best allow you to express your passion, values, strengths and purpose and how you can connect more strongly to the things that give you meaning.

Passion – in what kinds of work are there opportunities to get paid for the things you are already passionate about? If you love gardening, could you get paid for doing other people's gardens?

What are my passions?	What kind of work would allow me to express my passions more fully?

Be careful, however, that turning your passion into paid work does not take away the fun. You may enjoy digging your own garden, but would you enjoy doing it as paid work for others?

One word of warning: just because you love doing something, even if you are good at it, does not mean it will necessarily make you rich or even enable you to earn a living.

Values – these are about what you believe in and think is important. It is unlikely you will enjoy a job that conflicts with your values. What kinds of work would most align with your values?

What are my values?	What kind of work would allow me to express my values more fully?

Strengths – in what kind of work will I have most opportunity to exercise my strengths, the things I am good at and enjoy?

What are my strengths?	What kind of work would allow me to exercise these strengths more often?

Purpose – what kind of work best aligns with my purpose in life?

What is my purpose?	What kind of work would allow me to express my purpose more fully?

Selecting different forms of work that suit you best

We will look at five of the most common contexts in which we work:

1. Improving your current job.

2. Looking for a new job.

3. Developing a side hustle alongside your existing job.

4. Trying out the gig economy.

5. Working full time for yourself.

IMPROVING YOUR CURRENT JOB

You may already have a job you enjoy on balance but which could be improved, or you may not be willing to take the risk of moving to a new role or new organization. In this case, you can still use the principles from Chapter 4 to continue to improve your current job.

If you are a little dissatisfied and thinking of making a change, it makes sense to start by trying to improve your current role. Even if you are unhappy with your current work, or thinking of quitting, you have nothing to lose by trying to redesign your job. It is usually easier to redesign what you have than to start over in a new organization, where you may find you face the same problems.

You usually have valuable resources, relationships and knowledge in your current job and organization that you can use as a springboard to make things better. Part of this is also about starting to evolve your current role in the direction that will meet your career goals or help you build skills to take the next step. This gives you an opportunity to continuously reinvent and evolve your career before someone else does it for you without your input.

In the last chapter, I identified some principles for reengineering your work to increase your engagement at work. If you did not already try these as you read Chapter 4, start by applying these exercises to your current role:

- How can you spend more time on the parts of the job that give you meaning and less on the parts that do not?

- How can you design more meaning and engagement into your current job?

- How can you reengineer your tasks, relationships, mindset and location to make your job more fulfilling and enjoyable?

LOOKING FOR A NEW JOB

If you really do not enjoy your job and do not think it can be repaired, then before looking for another job it is important to be clear about the source of your dissatisfaction. Otherwise, you risk jumping from one unsatisfactory job to another.

As in Chapter 4, use the framework of tasks, relationships, mindset and location to think about your specific source of dissatisfaction and the solutions. For example:

- If you do not enjoy the tasks and cannot find a way to reengineer them, then it is no use looking for a new job in the same area as the tasks will be similar – you need a career change.

- If you do not like your boss or colleagues, your motivation may be to get away from them rather than the work itself or the organization. If you like the organization otherwise, then start looking for a new job internally.

- If you do not like the company culture, then you need to join another organization.

- If you do not like the location or the commute, you can request flexible working or find a job with a remote work option or in a location that works better for you.

- If the problem is your pay, then you have nothing to lose by asking for a pay rise before you decide to leave.

If absolutely everything is dreadful, be careful that the problem is not you. Your attitude and mindset are things you carry with you wherever you go and will shape your experience of whatever job you try.

On social media I often observe that a high proportion of commenters seem to have had consistent and extremely negative experiences of every job, group of colleagues and boss they have ever had. If you always have terrible jobs and bad relationships, then the common denominator might be you!

Use the exercise above to identify the kind of work that is likely to allow you to:

- live your values

- exercise your strengths

- pursue your passions

- live your purpose.

It is unlikely that any one job will allow you to do all these things and it may be that you need a balanced portfolio of leisure, work and other activities to engage all the elements and bring you meaning. This might mean a significant change and could require retraining or a move to a role with lower levels of compensation initially.

Usually, it is not a good idea to quit before you have found another

role – employed people get more interviews and get three times more
job offers than unemployed ones.

DEVELOPING A SIDE HUSTLE ALONGSIDE YOUR EXISTING JOB

You may not be ready to jump from a full-time job into something
completely different, but there are ways to experiment and try out
different things alongside a full-time job. The idea of a side hustle is
to do something on top of your main job.

We live in an era of unparalleled opportunity to develop new gigs
and side hustles. We do not even need to leave the house to start drop
shipping (marketing or selling a product where fulfilment is done by
someone else) or affiliate marketing. Anyone with a smartphone can
sell digital content, transcribe speech, be a virtual assistant or an online
influencer.

You can easily find examples of people earning a living (sometimes
a fortune) as food bloggers or fashion influencers, eyebrow models or
product unboxers. People are being paid for playing e-sports, travel
blogging, streaming videos of them playing games or listening to music.
Anything that attracts eyeballs can be monetized through advertising
or sponsorship. The opportunities are limited only by our imagination
and our ability to create compelling content and develop followers.

If you are not interested in becoming an online influencer, you could
set up a small business or activity you do in your free time. You could
take a second job to earn an extra income, learn new skills or try out
a different environment. You could start to do something you find
personally fulfilling or try out a new skill or sector.

There are several online global marketplaces such as Upwork, Guru
and Toptal where you can register your skills and be contacted by
people who have a need. At my companies I often use freelancers
through these sites for research or for specific projects in areas like
marketing support. If you want to try exercising your skills in a different
environment or see whether your business idea works, these platforms
offer a low-cost, minimal-risk way for you to start by bidding on small
projects where you know you can do an excellent job at a reasonable
price.

Focus initially on building your reputation and overdelivering on
your commitments to make sure you get good feedback (even if you
do not make much money at this stage). You can fine tune your offer
as you work out what you enjoy and what you like and dislike about
the work. You can refine the way you work to improve your outputs

and to deliver faster and better. As you build your reputation you can bid for larger pieces of work, push your pricing and try out new ideas. If it is something you want to develop further, continue to build reviews, then pick a slightly more challenging project and/or push up your pricing a bit.

At all times you remain in control of how much work you accept. If you find you enjoy it and there is a big demand for the skills you have, you might find you are spending more time on these activities. They could even become your main source of income.

These platforms can be a useful way of prototyping a business idea if you are planning to offer a service. You can give it a go and see if the demand is there. You might find that the income and engagement you get through this route is enough for you. If there is good demand and you want to grow, you might want to take the next step and develop it into a fully fledged business.

You can go on these sites and look up the kind of work available and how much it pays. As with a full-time job though, make sure it speaks to your values and purpose and allows you to exercise your strengths. Adding another job you do not really like to your existing one is not going to improve your average happiness.

TRYING OUT THE GIG ECONOMY

Some side hustles develop into full-time activities, some people may combine several smaller jobs or income streams to get the variety, flexibility and income that they need. In the gig economy people tend to be self-employed and do a range of things.

Some commentators estimate that up to 50 per cent of all work will be freelance within 20–30 years. This is unlikely, but there will be an increase in the availability of this kind of work.

The 'gig economy' can include anything from on-call temporary workers to zero-hours contracts, to Uber and food delivery drivers, to people working online through freelance platforms like Upwork. In the gig economy, people's entire work is a combination of different gigs. The original members of the gig economy of course were artists such as musicians, actors or other performers.

While there are, of course, disadvantages to these kinds of temporary work, and challenges with income and security, they do allow us to spread our risk across multiple streams of income. It may seem as though you have more security in a full-time job, but if that disappears for some reason you go from 100 per cent to 0 per cent security instantly.

If you have a range of options, you can switch between them to balance your needs.

The gig economy also offers flexibility for people who do not want, or are unable to commit to, a single way of spending their time or a sole source of income. However, I should add a note of caution: the gig economy can be great for people who actively choose it but according to McKinsey, most independent Gen Z workers still say they would prefer to work as a permanent employee.

You may want to start out with a side hustle gig and then build on it progressively if it works for you. Alternatively, if you find yourself without a job and needing some income, there is little downside in trying this out.

WORKING FULL TIME FOR YOURSELF

The highest risk, and the highest potential reward, is working full time for yourself. About 15 per cent of people in the UK and 6 per cent in the USA are self-employed. Many people are attracted by the autonomy of being their own boss and shaping their own future.

In general, people working for themselves in the UK earn more per hour than people doing the same job working for someone else. The downside is that the number of hours you get to work may be more variable and you may have to do a lot of work in marketing and administration that does not get paid, so you need to allow for this in your calculations.

You will also not get paid holidays, parental leave or sick pay and you should expect challenges in managing work–life balance. If you are working on your own, then if you are not working you are usually not earning.

Researchers from the universities of Sheffield and Exeter studied 5,000 workers in the UK, USA, Australia and New Zealand across many sectors and levels. Across the board the self-employed were happier at work even though they worked longer hours. They mentioned that freedom and control over their work significantly boosted their happiness and work satisfaction. Other surveys have found consistently that the self-employed are happier at work even when they may not earn as much as they would as employees in the same role and often experience greater uncertainty.

However, there is a relatively high risk that your business idea will not work out: in the UK about 60 per cent of businesses fail within the first three years. Only one in three make it to 10 years.

I do not say this to put you off – I made the decision to move out of the corporate world and work for myself. However, I think you need to do it with an open mind and a realistic assessment of the risks.

It is not within the scope of this book to offer a template for setting up your own business or scaling it, but if you are thinking of doing this, I would suggest beginning with the following steps:

1. **Define your goal in having a business.** How does it fit into your life? There is a significant difference between founding a business for just yourself at age 60 with the intention of doing some interesting work for a few years and founding a business in your 30s with the intention of growing a team and a brand over the next decades. The routes and risks you take will be fundamentally different.

2. **Find your idea.** What problem are you solving and for whom? Who would be prepared to pay for it and how much? You can take some of the risk out of this by considering a franchise from an existing company that has done the work in advance. This should give you a lot of support in getting started, but remember that your rewards will be shared with the franchisor.

3. **Put together an initial business plan.** A quick online search will show you lots of articles, formats and books on this topic. The discipline of constructing a business plan and in particular thinking about who your customers are, how you are going to get money from them and how much it is going to cost you to do that will really help focus your mind.

4. **Test your ideas.** Do some informal market research with people you know, research other businesses that are doing something similar, or use some of the ideas above to test out your ideas as a side hustle or on a freelance basis.

5. **Many people start a business because they love the product or the service they plan to supply.** It is a great start if you are passionate about doing the work, whether it be making stone fireplaces or providing accountancy services. However, just doing the work is not enough. If you have your own business you will need to master marketing and sales and you will also need to

allocate time for invoicing, tax returns, chasing payments and endless government bureaucracy. You may well find that less than half of your time is available for doing the work you enjoy. In the early days you will do the work full time and then move on to the administration in the evenings and at weekends. Be honest about your willingness, skills and the time all of this will take in your business plan.

6. Consider how you are going to find customers. How will you communicate with them, convince them and close the sale?

If your idea survives these initial questions, then it is time to get some advice on how to structure and register your business and to think about company names, websites, etc. It is an exciting time and I wish you good luck with it. I do not regret going down that route.

UNPAID WORK AND VOLUNTEERING

Many people get a great deal of personal satisfaction from volunteering. It can help you contribute to society, build new skills and meet new people. Others have decided to prioritize family or caring responsibilities which are not paid.

According to NCVO, a membership community for charities, voluntary organizations and community groups in England, about 40 per cent of people had volunteered in some way in the last 12 months. Of those, 65–74 year olds were the most active volunteers, 25–34 year olds the least, reflecting their different amounts of time available after traditional work. Most are motivated by a desire to do good or to support a cause that is important to them.

Because this type of work is purely voluntary it should always be about something that brings you meaning, fulfilment and happiness. If you can exercise your skills for the benefit of others, most people find this very motivating.

Again, if you go back to your purpose, your passions, your values and your strengths, these should give you ideas about sectors or tasks where you feel you want to contribute. There are several online platforms that connect volunteers with opportunities to volunteer – just search for 'volunteering'. Browsing these can generate even more options. One UK source I found had over one million opportunities to help.

Volunteering can be a fantastic way of exercising a skill or an aspect of your identity that you do not get to fulfil in other areas of your life.

- What part does volunteering play in your portfolio career?

- Which areas do you feel drawn to volunteering in?

- What skills can you bring?

- What do you want to get out of the experience?

- How could you try this out?

Elements of a great work portfolio

If you find one job that satisfies all your needs and gives you sufficient life meaning, then you are incredibly lucky. Many people need to put together several work and leisure activities to fulfil all their needs. In a portfolio career it is the blend that gives you total satisfaction – no individual part of it must do everything, although they should each be congruent with some of your values. These complementary elements give you variety and insurance against temporary setbacks in any one area. That is why many great wines are blends.

A good portfolio career will usually include:

- at least one 'no brainer' reliable source of work that helps pay the bills

- several customers, otherwise you are just employed in a different form

- at least one thing you really love, even if it does not pay

- a focus on spending time doing what you enjoy doing – do not get sidelined into things that are not really you just because they are available

- a blend that overall engages most of your values, strengths, passion and purpose.

You might find that available generic job roles provide at least part of your portfolio, such as part-time work doing what you already do, consulting, freelancing or volunteering around your existing role and skill set – if you enjoy it.

If you are doing work you are passionate about, you are likely to be good at it, but it does not necessarily mean other people will want to pay for it.

As well as working for other organizations, there is a huge demand for individual and personal services from everyone from plumbers to personal trainers and coaches. Are there things you could do that could sell to individuals as well as organizations?

Can you turn your passion into something that others will pay for? If you enjoy house decorating, for instance, could you be paid for doing it for others? But be careful that your passion does not become work and you lose the enjoyment.

Making the change to a portfolio career is a major life transition for you and for people close to you – it will define the quality of 40 per cent of your waking hours for as long as you work. It is worth spending some time and thought on getting this right.

CHAPTER 6

Positive Relationships

* * *

Having positive relationships and connections with others is an important element of wellbeing and has an impact on all areas of life, work and leisure. People with satisfying relationships with other people experience longer and healthier lives, better brain function and higher levels of life satisfaction.

However, we do not always have the relationships we need. UK surveys find that between 23 and 33 per cent of adults in the UK 'always or often' feel lonely. Isolation poses a greater risk to health than obesity and has an impact equivalent to smoking 15 cigarettes a day. It is also associated with a 50 per cent higher risk of developing dementia.

Most adults spend roughly equal amounts of time in three social contexts:

- with strangers or co-workers in public spaces

- with family

- alone.

To be happy and fulfilled we need to be comfortable in all three of these contexts. In this section, I will focus on the first two contexts. Chapter 7 and Chapter 8 can give some more ideas on what to do when you are alone.

In later life we tend to spend an increasing amount of time alone, so we need to put the work in to develop both relationships and interests in advance of this.

Loneliness is a feeling that we do not have the social connections we want (so it varies a lot between individuals) and is meant to prompt us to action – to reach out and connect. We should see it as a spur to action, not a state of being.

Of all the things we do, interactions with others are usually the least predictable and have a big impact on our mood and thoughts. Human beings are very attuned to relationships and the feedback we receive from other people. Being with other people gives us an external focus and goal to navigate rather than falling back inside our own heads.

The Greek word 'idiot' originally meant someone who lived by themselves. The Greeks assumed that someone who cut themselves off from community interaction would be mentally incompetent.

Although we know the importance of relationships instinctively, many of us go through periods of life where we have other priorities, we need to work and take the kids to school and activities. Life gets busy. During these stages it is easy to neglect friendships because spending time with friends is a voluntary activity in amongst all the other urgent things that demand our time.

Many of us are dissatisfied with the amount of connection we have with others, but we often wait, passively hoping for connection to find us, for others to make the first move or to organize something. Our first tip here is that if you are dissatisfied with your relationships, you need to make a start rather than waiting for others.

In this section, I am going to identify some simple tools for analysing your key relationships and working to improve them where you want to do so. I will start with some principles and a relationship audit, then we will look at how you can improve the relationships you want to.

How many friends does one person need?

In his book *How Many Friends Does One Person Need?* anthropologist Robin Dunbar found that the maximum number of casual friends the average person can handle in their wider social network was 150. He also found that within this number we had 'rings' of successively more intimate groups, changing by a factor of around three each time.

- The next step down, 50, is the number of people we call friends – neighbours, work colleagues and acquaintances you might invite to a dinner. You see them often, but they are not close friends or true intimates.

- Then there is the circle of 10–15 people, the close friends that you can turn to for advice or sympathy and to confide in on most topics when you need to.

- The most intimate Dunbar number, in the range 3–6 people, is your close support group. These are your best friends and often family members.

I am going to focus on these three smaller groups in terms of developing our relationships as these have the biggest impact on our wellbeing and life satisfaction.

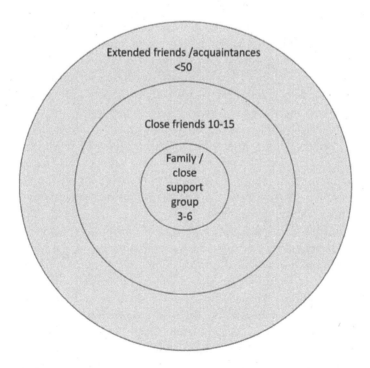

Note that these numbers are cumulative so the 15 number for close friends includes the 3–6 people in your close support network and so on. People can move between layers and sometimes fall out of them altogether. If you do not spend time on relationships, they will naturally decay over time.

Two factors define the level of intimacy in a relationship:

- How much time you spend with these people – on average we spend 40 per cent of our social time with our close support group and 20 per cent with our close friends. That is 60 per cent of our time with our closest 15 relationships. The quality of friendships is directly dependent on the time we invest in them.

- The nature and intensity of the shared experience – do we meet for a coffee, just say hi in the street or do something active and challenging together?

We can only hold a certain number of people at a particular intensity level. 'The amount of social capital you have is pretty fixed,' Dunbar says. 'It involves time investment. If you garner connections with more people, you end up distributing your fixed amount of social capital more thinly so the average capital per person is lower.'

We may have a small number of friends whose relationships survive infrequent contact and distance – usually people we had an intensive relationship and shared experiences with in the past.

On average people spend 20 per cent of their waking hours, or 3.5 hours per day, engaged in social interaction – eating or sitting with others, and talking. Dunbar found that these numbers also seemed to occur on social media, so a typical number of friends on Facebook is 150, but if we look at how many people we actively engage with daily, it is nearer to the 3–6 number.

Our friendship patterns are magnified by how we communicate through technology. For example, we tend to telephone the people we see most often as well.

Having said all this, people vary widely and it is not about hitting a target number of friends that you 'should' have, it is about having the number you want and the degree of emotional intimacy you seek. These needs can vary widely by individual.

Some researchers believe that we tend to put too much focus on seeking a small number of 'best friends' and not enough on the next group of 10–15 friends.

WHAT DOES THIS LOOK LIKE IN YOUR LIFE?
Here are some guidelines on how to categorize the people in your social life into these groups. They are very rough guidelines based on the research but will help clarify your thinking.

Group	Characteristics	How often we communicate
Close support group: 3–6 people	Give unhesitating emotional and financial support, lend household items, help with chores and companionship, fulfil intimacy needs.	At least once a week (often a lot more) and we feel emotionally close to them.
Close friends: the next group up to a total of 15 including your close support group	Most everyday social companions, they fulfil social needs and provide practical help and support.	On average we spend a couple of hours every other month with each.
Friends and acquaintances: up to 50 including the 3 groups above	Party friends you would invite to your birthday or a weekend event.	Contact at least once every six months.
Just friends: up to 150 including the groups above	People you would send Christmas cards to, extended family, children of close friends, work colleagues. People you exchange information with or invite to a once-in-a-lifetime event such as a wedding.	Once a year.

Researchers found differences in how different types of people build their networks.

- In studies of British and Belgian women, about half of their social network was made up of extended family.

- The bigger the family, the fewer outside family relationships.

- Women consistently have slightly more friends than men.

- Extraverts tend to have larger networks (but spend less time with each of them and therefore tend to have weaker and less supportive relationships) than introverts.

Each of these is just a different strategy to get the relationships you want and value.

How does your network of relationships look?

I have found that it is useful to visualize and audit your network to identify gaps and opportunities to improve.

To keep the numbers manageable for this exercise I would like you to focus on your close support group (the most intimate 3–6) and close

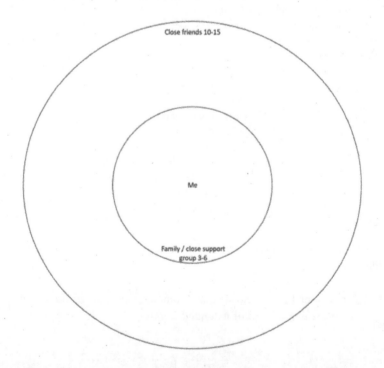

friends (the next 10–15). You can apply the same principles to your extended friendship group of up to 50 afterwards if you find this helpful.

Draw the circles above on a piece of paper. The circles represent the different levels of intimacy.

Now add the names of the people in your family/close support group in the inner circle and the names of the people in your close friends group in the outer circle. Spread them around so you will have space to add information on how they connect to you.

For each of these relationships, label it with four pieces of information:

- How important is the relationship to you? H/M/L (high, medium, low)

- How strong is the relationship now? S/N/W (strong, neutral, weak)

- How much time do you spend with them? (hours per week on average)

- What is the flow of communication between you? G/O/P (good, OK, poor)

If there is other information you think would be useful, such as how far away from you they live or shared interests, feel free to add it.

When you have finished it will look something like the diagram on the next page.

What do you notice about your map? Are there any gaps or concerns? A red flag is where there are particularly important relationships that are weak or where communication is poor.

I have also found that explaining your relationship map to another person really helps to bring it alive. This might be something you want to discuss with a partner or close friend.

Now, based on your analysis, choose which specific relationships you would like to improve.

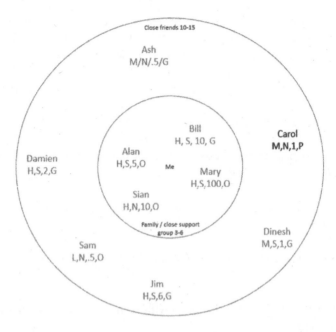

Use this table to think in more detail on your key relationships and goals for these relationships

Name	How would you describe the quality and nature of this relationship now?	What is your goal?

For many people, their relationships with their spouse or partner and close family will be among their most intense and important relationships. They can be either the most supportive or the most challenging when times are tough. If you have serious problems with these very close family relationships, I encourage you to get professional support.

For the purposes of these exercises, I will be assuming that these intimate relationships are OK and treating them in the same way as other close relationships. It is beyond the scope of this book to offer intensive couples or family counselling.

You might find the process of re-evaluating your life through this book and making some changes will require some discussion with your family and close friends. Your relationship with your partner can change and may need to evolve. As your purpose and how you spend your time change, you need to keep communicating about what you each want and how you feel about the changes.

THE SEVEN PILLARS OF FRIENDSHIP

Dunbar found that, in general, our friends tend to resemble us in many ways – we usually select friends based on how much we have in common with them. He calls this the Seven Pillars of Friendship and you are more likely to establish close friendships with people who share these factors:

1. Having the same language or dialect.

2. Growing up in the same location.

3. Having the same educational and career experience.

4. Having the same hobbies and interests.

5. Having the same worldview (moral, religious and political views).

6. Having the same sense of humour.

7. Having the same musical tastes.

The more boxes the friend ticks, the more time you will tend to spend with them.

We tend to share six or seven of these pillars with our inner five close support group members, but are likely to share only one or two with the outer layer of 150 friends – it does not matter which ones you share (according to Dunbar, one factor is not more important than others). In addition, positive relationships need to meet at least two conditions: some compatibility between our goals and being willing to invest attention in the other person's goals. We often spend more time with a new friend initially while we work out how much we share, then they settle back to the appropriate level for the longer-term relationship.

In general, our friendships tend to be with people of the same sex, ethnicity, age and often personality. For example, most people's social networks up to 150 tend to consist of 70 per cent the same gender; the cross-sex friends are often mainly, but not all, extended family.

We also tend to make more effort to see people and view them as important if they live within 30 minutes' travel (it does not seem to matter how far you travel, it is the time it takes). This, together with the other pillars, shows why moving to a new location can make building and maintaining relationships more challenging.

It also means that our natural networks tend not to be very diverse unless we work at it. Often the highest level of diversity is in our relationships at work where we are more likely to mix with people of different ethnicities, ages and social and economic backgrounds. If we want to maintain a diverse group of relationships, particularly if we are not employed, we need to work at it.

What makes a good relationship?

Our lives are heavily influenced by the quality of our close relationships, for good and bad. Be intentional about who you spend your time with and if necessary upgrade who is in your closest friend groups.

For the relationships you want to work on, ask yourself:

1. Do you feel energized when you are around them?

2. Do they encourage you or are they negative and critical?

3. Do they celebrate or begrudge your successes?

4. Do they stimulate you intellectually?

5. Do you encourage each other to grow and develop?

6. Is there a good balance of give and take?

7. Do they encourage healthy habits?

What are the qualities you most look for in a friend? Add these characteristics to the list above.

How do the people you want to improve your relationship with score against these qualities?

Do your closest five relationships support the person you want to be in the future or embody qualities you admire?

Now is the time to spend more time with people who build you up and less (or none) with people who drag you down. Remember, if you have a difficult relationship with one of your five closest friends, you are also one of their five closest, so you are partly responsible for how they behave! What is it you do that helps create or enable the behaviours you observe in them?

How do you score as a friend against the criteria above in their eyes? Maybe you should ask.

This is not about abandoning your oldest and closest friends because you want to meet people who are more attractive or richer, but it does involve getting rid of toxic relationships and replacing them with people who give you energy, build you up and help you grow. The same principle applies to other people and ideas that have an influence on you. The media you read, the people you see as role models, the time you spend on social media, etc. will all shape your mood, opinions and perspectives. Be careful what you let into your head, it shapes who you become.

CONNECT

In their book *Connect*, David Bradford and Carole Robin wrote about creating exceptional relationships. They identified a continuum from people who are just contacts without real connection through to relationships where there is an active attachment, and finally to reaching a relationship where you are really known, supported, affirmed and accepted.

The authors' checklist for exceptional friends is where:

- both can be fully themselves

- both are willing to be vulnerable

- you trust self-disclosures will not be used against you

- you are honest with each other

- you deal with conflict proactively

- both are committed to each other's growth and development.

They describe a process for how relationships develop. This process takes time – there is no such thing as instant intimacy.

1. The relationship starts with a common or complementary interest but does not feel the need to go deeper.

2. Some relationships develop to ones where they communicate more openly and deeply; people find more areas to connect and trust grows.

3. The people start to take more risks on what they disclose to each other and become more vulnerable.

4. The cycle reinforces itself, moving over time to being able and willing to discuss progressively deeper issues.

5. Obligations and expectations build. Points of difference need to be navigated. If this is done successfully, openness and honesty grow.

6. They learn how to influence each other and develop more interdependence.

7. To continue to grow requires more disclosure and risk taking and often progresses through one or more critical issues or conflicts.

For the relationships you want to develop, which of the seven stages are they at now and what would you need to do to advance them to the next stage? Remember, what works best depends on the other person too. Keep the focus on them as well as yourself.

Making new close friendships is difficult, not least because the other person is already embedded in their own existing networks of friends. Adding one more close friend would mean them giving up one of their existing ones. Apply this to the relationships you plan to improve.

Relationship	Which stage are you at now?	What will you do to advance to the next stage?	Is there anything you or they do that prevents this?

BILLY NO-MATES

In his excellent book *Billy No-Mates*, Max Dickins looks at some specific challenges for men in maintaining friendships and relationships.

Maintaining relationships is an issue for everyone, but divorce, bereavement and retirement tend to affect men more than women, partly because male friendships are often focused on work. In a heterosexual relationship, men often delegate the maintenance of their relationships to women, who are more likely to organize birthdays, social events and celebrations and keep up to date with the news about family and friends.

Dickins found that men often have several mates but few (half said they had none) who they would discuss serious topics like money or health with. Men's social circles also shrink more than women as they age, and women on average maintain and build new friendships more often.

He noticed that a lot of the literature on friendship focuses on talking about your feelings and sharing vulnerability, but that this works less well for men. Men are then criticized for not forming and maintaining relationships in the same way that women do.

According to a long study from Harvard from 1972 to 2004, the biggest factor that separated men who aged well and lived the longest from those that did not was the quality of their relationships.

It is doing stuff together that works best for men – it may be then that instead of focusing on building one-to-one relationships or openly discussing vulnerabilities and emotions, it is better to focus on recreating the contexts where male friendships happen. Focus on the context of what we do together – it is fundamentally about the time spent together and the consistency of contact.

Structure your opportunities to maintain friendships, for example organize a monthly pub visit to invite your friends. Why not ask them to bring a friend of their own they have not seen for a while?

It is not about getting men to behave like women or to form friendships in the same way that women do, it is about broadening your range of tools and the modes in which you can show up. It is about not being trapped in your stereotype of what you can and cannot do.

What are the contexts in which you can connect? What can you do together?	Who will you invite?	When will you start?

Chapter 7 will also give you some ideas for creating activities that bring opportunities to connect with different groups of people.

Tips for moving a friendship to higher levels of intimacy

As we have seen above, relationships often develop through increasing self-disclosure. There is of course a risk in over-sharing, but also in holding too many things back.

Bradford and Robin propose the '15 Percent Rule' to address this. If you are currently operating in what they call the 'Zone of Comfort', basing the relationship on things you feel safe doing or saying, the next move is pushing out into the 'Zone of Learning' where you are unsure of how the other person will respond.

What you want to avoid is straying into the 'Zone of Danger', discussing or doing things that would have negative repercussions. To avoid landing in the danger zone, they suggest expanding your comfort zone into the learning zone about 15 per cent at a time. With each success, open another 15 per cent.

1. If you are interested in a friendship, add a new context. If you work together, go to lunch or out for a drink. These things signal to people that you are interested in being friends with them – different conversations happen in different places.

2. Try to create contexts where you can do an activity together in a playful way – see the section on hobbies and interests for tips on creating fun.

3. Work on your listening skills. Listen for what people say and the emotions behind it. Check your understanding before responding. Make people feel heard.

4. If people are sharing their frustrations or feelings, ask for more. I slept badly, why was that? I have a headache, what brought that on? An empathic statement opens conversations and asks them to elaborate or go deeper with what they are saying. Telling your story closes this down. Talk less about yourself, ask them more questions. We need to restrain our own need to say something and concentrate on what the other person is trying to express.

5. Give time to the relationship – Jeffrey Hall from the University of Kansas found that it takes around 50 hours spent together to move people from being acquaintances to casual friends. It took 90 hours to become a 'friend' and more than 200 hours before you would normally call someone a close friend. How much time you spend with someone determines the intimacy you create.

6. Friendship is a rhythm and it is easy to fall out of it. Keep scheduling things over time or friendships will decay.

7. Ask specific questions showing that you know what is happening in their day, not just general ones.

8. Be present when you are with them – switch off distractions like phones.

9. Look for opportunities to give and take feedback or support.

10. Take a leap of faith and trust people. Increase your disclosure by 15 per cent.

Think about your own style and approach. Which of these tips do you think you and your relationships would benefit from trying? How will you do this?

Go back to the relationships you want to improve. What will you do next?

Relationship	What will I do next?

A NOTE ON RELATIONSHIPS AFTER RETIREMENT

During our working lives, many relationships are formed and maintained through working together. When we no longer share that common interest, some of these relationships fall away.

Work is also often where we form relationships with a much more diverse group of people than at home. Our outside work friends tend to be more homogeneous, for example of a similar age, background and ethnicity to ourselves.

It is worth thinking about the context in which you could create new relationships as you start to pull back from full-time work and mix with people who are different from yourself to preserve variety, particularly if this is something you enjoy in the work context. It is particularly healthy to maintain connections to younger people through multi-generational groups and interests.

FINDING YOUR TRIBE

From our first days at school, we tend to look for people who share common interests or possess the traits we aspire to adopt. Our tribe could be based around a common interest in sport or music, or it could be a physical community or based around practising a particular art or profession.

What are the common characteristics of the people you really enjoy spending time with outside of your family? What are they doing, how are they behaving? What were the communities or groups of people you have really enjoyed being part of in the past?

If you can see some consistent characteristics, these people might be your 'tribe'. Spending time with people in your tribe can be deeply satisfying.

- What do you think is your tribe?

- Where do they meet or spend time online?

- How can you get involved and connect with them more?

Revisiting your purpose, passions, values and strengths should give you some ideas around the kind of people that may form part of your tribe.

A warning: in the social media age you can find a tribe that gathers around any topic, both healthy and unhealthy. While it can be fun to mix with people who are like you already, it is also important to be open to connecting with people who are different. In building a healthy portfolio of relationships we need a balance between the two or we can be drawn into very insular worlds.

CONNECTING WITH YOUR BROADER COMMUNITY

Just as with financial investments, in social networks and relationships it is good to have a diversified portfolio.

'Weak ties' such as acquaintances and neighbours matter too and some may grow into stronger relationships in the future. These weak ties can also introduce new perspectives, ideas and information. Because our close friends tend to move in the same circles that we do, their perspectives and knowledge overlap with what we already know. Acquaintances are connected to people we do not know and know things that we do not.

If you found the relationship mapping exercise useful, you can extend it to the next group of up to 50 acquaintances and use the principles above to try to extend or deepen these relationships where you would like to.

- Which of your more distant acquaintances would you like to get to know better?

- How will you start?

See more ideas on what types of activities you could get involved in to develop new social connections in our next chapter on leisure, hobbies and interests.

Engaging Leisure and Interests

❖ ❖ ❖

It may seem a bit strange to talk about systematically planning your leisure. Many of us have hobbies or interests that have organically grown up over the years. The ones we find enjoyable we tend to do more of, the ones that lose our interest drift away. However, we also go through life stages where our time gets stretched by work, family or other commitments and sometimes we let things that we really like fall by the wayside. The things that nourish us can become depleted over time.

Time is the ultimate scarce resource, so how we choose to spend our time is the essence of a good life. Having more leisure time at your disposal, however, does not necessarily improve the quality of your life unless you know how to use it. Retirement can lead to depression, for example, and people report more illness on weekends and during holidays than when they are at work.

This chapter will give you some ideas on how to design a portfolio of leisure activities that are more enjoyable and fulfilling.

Our research shows that on average in industrialized countries we spend our waking time on the following activities:

1. Productive activities such as working (24–60 per cent) or, if we are in education, studying (20–45 per cent).

2. Maintenance activities (housework, grooming, eating): 20–42 per cent.

3. Leisure activities – media, hobbies, sports, socializing: 20–43 per cent.

The quality of our waking life consists of our experiences doing the three things above. Both what we do and how we do things matter.

Luckily, the world is full of interesting things to do, only a lack of imagination or energy stand in the way of creating a range of engaging leisure activities.

How you spend your time is the quality of your life, so improving your enjoyment of your leisure time can make a significant contribution. The 20–40 per cent of our time we spend on leisure includes activities such as consuming media, hobbies, sports and socializing.

Our hobbies and interests are also another channel to express our purpose, pursue our passions, live our values and exercise our strengths, as well as to reinforce the elements of a good life. For example, if one of your values is creativity but your work does not require much of this, then a highly creative hobby or interest may help you balance your portfolio. As you exercise your creativity more, you may find this starts to have an impact on other parts of your life.

If you are in the process of stepping back from full-time work, it may be tempting to do nothing for a while after decades of someone else structuring your diary, and it is not a bad idea to have a period of reflection and relaxation. However, a potential 30 years or more of retirement is too long for 'vacation mode' for most people.

Leisure and a lack of structure can be great in the short term but can lead to boredom and a lack of purpose over time. A 2019 UK survey by the British National Citizen Service mentoring group found that the average retiree grows bored after just one year. Boredom is a useful signal that you need to find the right pace for you personally. All life has a bit of boredom in it. The cure for boredom is not in just being mindlessly busy, it is about meaningful activity.

I will also encourage you in this chapter to try something new – an openness to new experiences is associated with increased life satisfaction among adults.

How do you spend your leisure time today?

In a typical week, how do you spend your leisure time? Include watching TV, browsing the internet or social media, sports, reading, socializing, relaxing and other hobbies. You might want to try keeping a diary or setting functions like screen time tracking on your phone to get accurate data.

Leisure activity	Time spent per week	Do you actively enjoy this/does it energize you?	Is that OK?

Great leisure activities are enjoyable and energize you – do your interests make you feel energized and create active enjoyment?

When you have done that, ask yourself if that is OK? Would you like to spend more or less time on this? Do you have enough variety in your leisure interests, are they enjoyable? Is anything obvious missing? Is there something you love doing that you are not making the time for?

Reduce passive consumption

The most common leisure activity for many people is watching television. Other screen time such as browsing the internet or social media is high on the list too.

After a busy day we may all need some time to veg out where we just put our feet up and relax without a lot of thought. However, these screen-based forms of leisure are designed to be addictive and it is easy to fall into spending more of your life than you wanted on watching detective series or cat videos or arguing with strangers online. People rarely report feeling actively energized or enjoying the experience of these passive activities. At best they tend to be neutral, at worst they create anxiety and anger.

How do you feel after an evening of watching TV or browsing social media? Are you energized, was it fun, did it give you positive energy? Or did you just lose yourself down a rat hole for an hour and cannot even remember what you did?

Try enabling screen time tracking on your phone to get a sense of how much time you are spending on that one screen alone – most people are surprised to find they are spending hours checking their phone.

Another good way of making phone time visible is to enable 'do not disturb' mode. We know that screen time just before bed tends to interrupt sleep by exposing you to light and content that may annoy you or over-stimulate your mind. Set your phone to automatically switch to 'do not disturb' mode an hour before you normally go to bed. For the first few days you will be constantly picking up your phone without really thinking and noticing that it asks you whether you want to proceed. Just that prompt will encourage you to leave it alone.

It is also a good practice to leave your phone out of reach when you go to sleep so that checking it is not the first thing you do when you wake up.

How much time do you spend watching television? The average person in the UK watches 22.5 hours of television per week. Whenever we say this, people are shocked and resistant to the statistic, but this is only equivalent to having the TV on from around 7 to 10 pm every day. After a typical evening of TV do you feel energized and fulfilled? Can you even remember the next day what you watched?

A common barrier to introducing new hobbies and interests is that we say we do not have enough spare time. Reducing screen time is a great place to start.

Where possible we should be looking to reduce the amount of time we spend on passive consumption activities and replace them with more active forms of leisure. This does not mean we should be rushing around all the time, but we should be finding a balance that creates active enjoyment, not passive mindlessness (unless that is what you want for a while).

Measure your screen time, then take one hour a day of TV/screen time and switch it to a more active pursuit – read a challenging book, take some exercise, play a game. Include some things that keep you mentally stimulated, such as playing cards, learning a language or doing puzzles.

If you normally switch the TV on at 7 pm, leave it switched off until 8 pm tonight. Invest your time in doing things that give you more energy. If that works, try switching another hour.

Hobbies and interests

Hobbies and interests should be fun – pick ones that make you happy.

- A hobby is something you do in your free time that brings you pleasure.

- An interest is a specific area where you are keen to learn more.

We often think of hobbies as something for people who live quiet lives with plenty of time for leisure, but people with busy and even stressful lives may need hobbies even more. Hobbies can provide a period of work-free time focusing on something completely different in a busy schedule.

Interests bring new learning and can help us develop or rekindle the habit of learning in other areas as well. Many hobbies and interests are social and bring us into contact with a different group of people than those we may meet at home or at work.

Many of us over time have lost track of what we like to do and what our interests are because we are busy doing other things, such as raising a family or working. In a balanced portfolio life, we may want to re-introduce variety in this area.

Think about those of your values that are not expressed enough elsewhere in your portfolio of activities, particularly meaningful hobbies or interests, which often include one or more of the following:

- Just having fun.

- Exercising your strengths.

- Connecting with your passions and the things you enjoy.

- Expressing an important value that is not expressed elsewhere.

- Learning something new.

- Staying well.

- Meeting a challenge or goal.

- Connecting with other people.

- Doing something that benefits others.

But of course, as always, it is up to you. It depends on your goals and preferences – do something that you will enjoy, not what other people are doing or that others think is meaningful or worthwhile.

WHICH HOBBIES OR INTERESTS SHOULD I CHOOSE?

You may already have a compelling hobby or interest (even a passion) that you plan to spend more time on. The challenge then is usually about carving out the time to do so. I will offer some tips on this in the section on action planning.

You may have had a past hobby or interest, as a child or as an adult, that you have allowed to lapse and would like to rekindle. What were the hobbies that brought you joy when you were younger that you stopped doing?

How can you restart them?

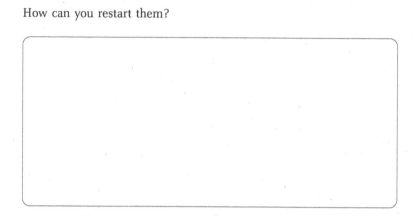

New hobbies may give you an opportunity to balance the expression of your values, raise your satisfaction in life segments you want to work on and build aspects of a fulfilling portfolio that might not be available in other areas. Remember, these activities are going to take up part of your valuable time – do not drift into things but plan them as part of your portfolio.

There is no need to rush into anything. Spend some time reflecting on the questions below and do some research. As you do this it might be useful to have open on screen a list of potential activities to spark ideas – search for 'list of hobbies and interests' and you will find hundreds of options.

When I was exploring other hobbies and interests, I used a directory of craft courses in the UK to identify a range of experience days and went on to try blacksmithing, woodturning, wood carving and glass blowing in addition to my usual interests such as motorsport with friends. I also went back to some of the things and people I enjoyed in the past and revisited them.

CHOOSE HOBBIES THAT EXPRESS OR SUPPORT YOUR PURPOSE, PASSIONS, VALUES AND STRENGTHS

Review the work you did on purpose, passions, values and strengths. Take the opportunity to think about any of these that have not been expressed in the other areas of your portfolio:

- What hobbies would support your purpose or passions and give you more enjoyment?

- What hobbies would be consistent with your values?

- What hobbies would allow you to use your strengths more?

- Which hobbies and interests can help you develop or express the key areas of wellbeing and happiness?

Questions	Hobby or interest ideas
Do you already have a compelling hobby or interest (maybe it is related to your passion)?	
Which hobbies would support your enjoyment, even develop it into a passion?	
Which hobbies would allow you to express your values (particularly ones which are not fully expressed elsewhere)? Your values	

Questions	Hobby or interest ideas
Which hobbies would allow you to use your strengths more often? Your strengths	
Which hobbies and interests can help you develop or express the key areas of wellbeing and happiness? Search for meaning Positive relationships Positive emotions Engagement/flow Accomplishment	

Reinforce the elements of a good life

If you found the elements of a good life (which include leisure) a useful checklist of areas to focus on, you can consider hobbies that reinforce one or more of the other elements as well.

If your hobby helps you to learn new things, meet new people and stay fit at the same time then it is reinforcing several other important parts of your portfolio. Look for activities that give you multiple benefits.

Hobbies can even spill over into your career, enabling you to develop new skills that you can then bring into your work and may even help with your financial wellbeing – however, it then starts to become work rather than leisure and recreation.

The elements	Hobbies and interests that would help support these
Meaningful 'work'	
Lifelong learning	
Engaging leisure and interests	
Positive relationships	
Physical and mental health and wellbeing	
Financial wellbeing	

SOME OTHER QUESTIONS THAT MAY PROMPT IDEAS

What kinds of people would you like to spend time with? What hobbies do they have? If all that seems too measured and sensible, what would take you well outside your comfort zone?

MAKING EVERYTHING FUN

In her book *The Power of Fun* Catherine Price writes about 'true fun'. True fun is something that happens in the moment, not a permanent state of being. Because of this, finding and creating situations that are fun is a much more practical goal than the less tangible one of 'being generally happy'. Laughter is often the best indicator – it marks the moment at which enjoyment has become true fun.

What are the contexts in which you find yourself laughing and having pure fun?

Where were you?	What were you doing?	Who else was there?

The author identifies three key factors that tend to characterize true fun:

- **Flow** requires us to be fully present and not distracted, using our skills and capabilities to overcome a challenge. We can only really focus on one thing at a time. You can see more on the concept of flow in Chapter 2. This is an important concept in several elements of building a portfolio life. Hobbies and interests are primarily things that we enjoy and get us into flow. Sometimes they lead to connection and playfulness, but flow is usually the initial condition.

- **Playfulness** is an attitude, a way of doing things. Play depends not on the activity but on the attitude we bring to it – do we use our imagination, are we silly, do we enjoy the absurd, spontaneous or uncertain? Do we let go of control?

- **Connection** means doing things with other people. Laughter is 30 times more likely to happen in a social context than when we are alone.

We can use these factors as a checklist to help actively design situations which are more likely to become fun.

Pick three leisure or other activities where you think you have fun. Which of the three factors above do you think are present at these times? If your hobbies engage just one of the three factors, how could you engage one more? If they engage two, how could you engage the third?

Activity	Fun factor 1: Flow	Fun factor 2: Playfulness	Fun factor 3: Connection	How can we engage more of the fun factors in this?

For example, if you find something that really challenges you and brings you into a state of flow, can you do it with other people and find a way to do it more playfully to engage all three of the factors? If you have great connection and playfulness with your friends in the pub, is there a challenge you could do together that would add flow to the experience?

Seek out sustained fun, but short micro-doses and boosters are worth pursuing. Even fleeting positive connections, such as a humorous inter-action with people when ordering a drink in a coffee shop, have been shown to improve mood.

Be proactive; do not wait for someone else to do it for you. What could you organize in future that has the potential to spark true fun? Think about what, where and who with.

If you like this idea you might want to add these factors to your daily or weekly audit. Write down three things you did today/this week to be playful, connected and/or in flow. How can you add in the other factors in future?

Trust your physical responses in determining whether something is fun to do. If you are asked to do something and your physical reaction is a tightening or tension in your body, or a feeling of restricted breath, say no. If it gives you a feeling of lightness and energy, say yes. Follow your energy.

Finding flow in leisure

I have written about the concept of flow in Chapter 4. Flow tends to happen when we are in a high-skill/high-challenge situation. This can also happen during active leisure.

People feel best in flow, when they are fully involved in meeting a challenge, solving a problem, discovering something new. Most activities that produce flow also have clear goals, clear rules, immediate feedback – external demands that focus our attention and makes demands on our skills. These are usually absent in passive free time, although they do exist in active activities, games and organized sport.

Teenagers in a study experienced flow (high-challenge/high-skill moments) about 13 per cent of the time when watching TV, 34 per cent when involved in hobbies and 44 per cent when taking part in sports or games. Hobbies were 2.5 times more likely to produce a state of heightened enjoyment than TV. Active games and sports were three times more likely to produce this state.

Flow often happens when people are doing their favourite activity – driving, talking to friends and, surprisingly, often at work.

Without goals and people to interact with, most people begin to lose motivation and concentration. Then the mind wanders, often onto areas that cause anxiety.

Unfortunately, the activities that give flow take more 'activation time', more organization, preparation and attention, so people usually spend four times more time watching TV than doing the more active and enjoyable activities.

Passive leisure – just hanging out with friends, reading an unchallenging book, listening to music alone, watching TV, etc. – does not take effort or demand the exercise of skills or concentration. Passive leisure seldom causes anxiety and can provide relaxation, but it often devolves into apathy. You will not find much active enjoyment, but you do not have to commit to anything.

Relaxation is not bad, it is the dosage that matters. If passive activities become the main way you use your leisure time, then passivity can become a habit and this has an impact on your quality of life. The less you do, the less you can find the time to do anything.

If you want to increase your probability of experiencing flow during leisure activities, seek activities with a balance of high skill and high challenge, clear goals, rules and an opportunity for feedback, and do it together with other people.

TIPS FOR STARTING A NEW HOBBY

- Be realistic about the time, energy and cost you are willing and able to dedicate.

- Do not get carried away, do your research and try some sample activities.

- It can take a while to get up a learning curve and enjoy a new interest, so it is good to commit to doing something at least three times before you decide to pursue it or to abandon it.

- Remember that you do not have to do it perfectly, it is meant to be fun.

- Do not compare yourself to others who have been doing it much longer – remember, they were once beginners too. However, if you are a competitive person, finding people of a similar standard to you and competing against them can be fun.

- Read some blogs, books, articles to prepare yourself.

- If you are motivated by doing things with other people, join an online community, go to a class.

- Just start doing something.

PUSH YOUR BOUNDARIES
If you want to introduce a bit of crazy into the process, make a list of six things that really 'aren't you', things that take you out of your comfort zone, things you tell yourself you would never do (legal ones only please). Make a numbered list one to six, throw a dice and do whichever number comes up.

LANGUAGE MATTERS
Everybody thinks they should do more exercise and the word 'should' is part of the problem.

One of the reasons I do not include physical health and exercise in any detail in this book, even though it is one of the key elements in building a long and happy life, is that people in general already know what they should be doing. We know we should not smoke, we should take regular exercise, get enough sleep, etc. The problem is that many of us do not do it. It is not about the knowledge of what to do, it is about the motivation.

If you are using the word **should** about anything then the motivation is extrinsic – that is, the motivation is coming from outside yourself. It is coming from the advice of others, things you have read. etc. This requires 'push motivation' and for us to exercise willpower to do some-thing we do not genuinely want to do.

The key to maintaining a new regime is to make the motivations intrinsic, things you **want** to do, such as self-improvement, self-expression, future health, fun, doing something for others or enjoyment. Intrinsic motivation creates a pull, it is something that draws you to it. The key is to find things that you enjoy for the sake of doing them alone and would do even without extrinsic motivations.

If you keep putting things off or cannot maintain a routine, then it is likely that you have not found the intrinsic motivation that draws you into the activity yet.

The exercises in this section should have given you some insights into activities that appeal to your intrinsic motivation – what really matters to you. What hobbies would support your intrinsic motivations? What do you enjoy doing for its own sake?

I will talk more about overcoming barriers to action in Chapter 10 on action planning.

A note on travel

Most people like to travel when they can afford to. According to a Transamerica Center for Retirement Studies report in 2017, 63 per cent of Americans aged 50 and older said travel was an important retirement goal. When we are travelling for only a few weeks a year, relaxation and variety may be enough.

If you have an opportunity to travel, or leisure becomes a bigger part of your life, or you become dissatisfied with just lying on a beach on vacation, you may consider combining the travel experience with some of the interests and hobbies you identified above. Could you combine it with learning a language, playing a sport or meeting new people to increase your satisfaction during travel?

While I was writing this book my son spent some time working from Argentina. He took the opportunity to pursue some of his longstanding hobbies such as martial arts in a new place, but also tried some new activities which are best explored in Buenos Aires, such as tango and polo.

Getting enjoyment from everyday maintenance tasks

On average people spend as much time on everyday maintenance activities such as cooking, grooming and housework as they do on leisure. We may not think of these as leisure, but there are opportunities to bring enjoyment into these activities as well, even to develop them into a hobby or interest.

Housework, personal care and idling are the activities that people report to be the least enjoyable experiences in their day. There is clearly a difference between cooking an everyday meal because your family are hungry and enjoying the process of creating a special meal or trying something new. However, we can turn cooking into a hobby, learn more about it, try more challenging recipes, work with other people and change the way we feel about it.

Are there ways you could take some of your everyday maintenance activities and turn them into something more enjoyable and recreational? I made the everyday experience of shaving more pleasurable by buying a beautiful mother-of-pearl-handled razor and luxurious shaving brush. I turned the daily experience of shaving into a short mindfulness exercise focusing on the sensations of shaving. I also bought an attractive Japanese teapot and cups and several types of loose-leaf tea, as well as attending a Japanese tea ceremony workshop to bring a little more pleasure into each time I have a cup of tea.

These are just two simple examples, but together they bring seven or eight small moments of pleasure into an average day. What could you do to make your everyday maintenance tasks more enjoyable?

PREPARING YOUR LEISURE PORTFOLIO FOR AGEING

As you age you may find it more difficult to do some physical activities and it is a good idea to build a selection of interests, things you can do on your own or with others, and things that you can do when you are physically active, as well as things you can do without needing to be so mobile or energetic.

If all your interests require a high level of mobility, such as active sport, you will struggle if mobility becomes a problem. It is good to have a range of other activities already in place to fall back on if this happens.

My father was a keen sportsman and most of his hobbies focused on being outdoors in nature. When he damaged his knee badly soon

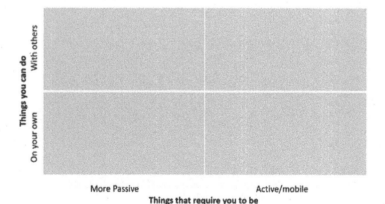

after retirement, he was unable to pursue the things he had always enjoyed and did not have much to fall back on.

From all the questions and exercises above, what are the criteria that make a good hobby or interest for you? What hobbies or interests would you like to rekindle or try that would fit these criteria?

What criteria would make a good activity for you?	What would you like to try that fits these criteria?

MOVING INTO ACTION

Try a couple of things, do more of what you enjoy and cut out activities that are passive.

How can you develop your current leisure time, hobbies and interests to make them more engaging and fun?

What new leisure activities will you try as an experiment?

In Chapter 10 I will give some tips on finding the time, getting started and building new habits.

CHAPTER 8

Lifelong Learning

* * *

Why is learning important enough to have a separate section of its own?

You may find it surprising that the area of learning has its own section in this book. It is not as obvious as work or leisure as a major aspect of our lives. To me, learning is not about sitting in a dusty classroom, it is the process of staying curious throughout our lives and constantly building our capability to move from where we are now to where we want to be.

Learning is a large part of the motivation and the skill set we need to make the changes in life we aspire to. If you think about the ideas you already have about how you want to change, what do you need to learn to implement the portfolio life you want?

As Gandhi said, 'Live as if you were to die tomorrow, learn as if you were to live forever.'

Learning can be something we get out of the way of – we expect to learn when we are young, but it is a tragedy if we stop learning when we are older. At the toddler stage children ask 'why' constantly. Richard Harris, a Harvard child psychologist, calculated that a child asks about 40,000 questions between the ages of two and five, that is about 100 a day. But then that number starts to fall dramatically and by the age of 18 most of us have stopped asking the 'why' question altogether.

There is little evidence that we lose our ability to learn as we get older, but we may lose our curiosity about a wide range of subjects. When did you last learn something new? I am not asking about just coming across new information but learning 'how' to do something new or differently, learning a new skill, language or other capability.

Lifelong learning and seeking proficiency are powerful drivers of self-esteem and engagement. However, a EU Labour Force Survey found that only 12 per cent of EU adults aged 24–64 had participated in 'lifelong learning' in the previous four weeks.

As we age, our curiosity remains, but we tend to focus on a narrower and narrower range of topics we find of use or interest. Our capability to learn remains, but many of us choose to use it less. We can, however, actively prime our curiosity to search more widely.

Developing a portfolio life and career is about exercising choice. To exercise choice, we need to learn new information, exercise judgement in new areas, build confidence and develop new skills. All of these depend on our ability to learn.

Improving your ability to learn can delay brain ageing and applying that ability can help you develop in all the other areas of life we have been exploring.

- It can support your search for meaning, passion and purpose.

- It can help you develop your strengths.

- It can help you build knowledge and skills about how to live all the elements of a good life (hopefully you have been experiencing this already in this book).

As we focus on any segment of our life and start to pay active attention to it, we can generate a potentially infinite range of opportunities for learning and action.

We also live in a period of rapid change, particularly in technology. We need to retain the ability to learn, adapt and unlearn some of our old practices throughout our career and life. If we want to remain relevant and up to date, learning is the key.

THE LEGACY OF FORMAL EDUCATION

We will each have had different experiences of school and other educational institutions. For many people, the process consisted of a systematic narrowing of the things they were told they were good at or allowed to study.

I learned I was supposedly 'bad' at languages, art and several sports. In later life I found I was quite good at most of these things if they were taught in a way that suited me and if my motivation was right. I had to choose at age 16 between arts and sciences, both of which I enjoyed. I chose arts topics and never really got back into practical science (though I remain fascinated by many scientific topics).

Formal education often leaves us with a legacy of learning to meet someone else's goal, to follow someone else's curriculum and to be tested against someone else's view of what is important. The methods of teaching used in most schools were not designed for you personally but to cope with typical learning styles and pace, and are often out of date with best practice.

However, you may have had the experience of finding something you really enjoyed and a teacher that really motivated you. If you did, this is likely to have stayed with you for the rest of your life. As an adult you now get to choose your learning goals, seek out your teachers and learn in a style and at a pace that suits you. The flipside of this freedom is that learning is now much more reliant on your personal drive and commitment than when you were spoon-fed information by others. You cannot blame your teachers anymore and it is down to you if you do not do the work.

Ideally, we will all build the mindset of learning for the love of it, not for financial gain but to express our values, deepen understanding and improve ourselves. But the goal is up to you – you might just want to learn to get better at poker! Follow your energy.

What do you want to learn?

Staying curious is key to initiating learning. As we age, inquisitiveness tends to fade; our ability to learn does not.

Curiosity is a survival aid, a hard-wired natural motivation to find out about new things. Neuroscience has found that when we are curious, our brain anticipates a reward in discovering the answer and gives us a dopamine shot when we do. We get an actual physical rush from learning something new.

As Ellen Parr puts it, 'The cure for boredom is curiosity, there is no cure for curiosity.'

Curiosity and learning are essential tools in managing life transitions, change and new challenges where we may need new perspectives, new skills or to take different types of actions. There is an exceptionally good chance that people have gone through these life stages or challenges before, that academics have studied them and that authors have written about them. You can benefit from what they learned and apply their ideas to your own situation.

Curiosity is often sparked by uncertainty or novelty. We tend not to be curious about topics we have not been exposed to already, so stimulating our curiosity usually means looking into new areas and trying new things.

As you start to imagine your new portfolio future, where are the gaps and new subjects you need to learn more about? What are the things you have long been curious about but have not had the time to investigate?

You may have already identified a few things you need to learn from the previous sections in this book. Here are some topics it might be good to be curious about (do you feel you have the knowledge and skills you need in these areas?):

- how to master your purpose and passions

- how to further develop your strengths

- getting better at your existing work or preparing for the next stage of your career

- mastering your hobbies and interests

- sustaining physical and mental health and wellbeing

- personal finance – how to budget, invest and make the best of your financial resources

- your stage of life (and the next one) – understanding and dealing with the challenges of this stage of your life – parenthood, work, relationships, retirement, etc.

But that is just what I think – what are you are curious about?

I have a notes page on my phone and if something strikes me as interesting and I would like to find out more, I make a quick note if I have not got time to investigate it at that moment. Alternatively, I type the question into a search engine and then email myself the link to the search page, so when I click back on it I am straight into resources that start to answer the question.

What is your learning goal?

From the work you have already done in working through the exercises and ideas in this book, choose one thing you would like to learn more about. This will give you a focus for the next parts of this chapter, which are about how to structure and accelerate your learning.

It can be both fun and challenging to choose something where you are a complete beginner – that is when you learn the most. To keep it simple, think about something that:

- you can learn near you or online, so it is easy to begin

- is not too time consuming, at least initially, so the barrier to starting is small

- is something you **want** to learn (not something you just feel you **should**)

- ideally is in an area where you will never be finished learning (so there is plenty of scope to continue if it captures your interest).

It should be something you have a genuine desire and motivation to learn about. This helps you overcome inertia to start and stay motivated to continue. Ask yourself, 'If I knew more about this or built that skill, what would I do differently in my life as a result?'

It can be useful to visualize in detail the end state of your learning, feel what it is like to be able to speak that language fluently or play a better game of tennis. The more real you can make your visualization, the better your motivation to learn.

One thing I would love to learn more about	Why? What will I do with this learning?

It is perfectly OK to be curious just for the sake of curiosity and interest, to follow your energy and have fun, but your motivation to learn will be higher if you have an active intention to do something with the learning. Having a goal helps you organize the mass of information you will encounter, focus on what is relevant and give it meaning for you. If you read a book with a goal in mind, for example, you will quickly spot the things that are relevant and will be more likely to recall and use them.

Now let us get started

Momentary curiosity is not enough. Things do not become interesting until we allocate time and attention to them. If we do not start to find out something more about it, we will forget about it – curiosity wanes without action.

There are two basic ways we can learn:

- Intuitively: we can just try things through repeated experience, successes and mistakes. There is a place for this once we get into practising what we have learned, but this tends to be a slow way of exploring all our options.

- Intentionally: through deliberate exposure to new knowledge and skills with the intention of learning and then reflecting on what we have learned – this is the approach we will follow.

It has never been easier to learn and access information about anything we are interested in: books can be downloaded instantly; searches, websites, blogs and global experts are a couple of clicks away 24 hours a day. We can quickly find local or online classes, videos, mentors and communities of practice and try things for ourselves.

Consider the difference in learning a language today versus 50 years ago. At that time, we had books or language teachers at school, we could record things on cassette, but there was little use of audio at that time. Today we have gamified apps to learn vocabulary, get feedback on our pronunciation and instantly translate words both ways. We have audio and video online lessons. We can use our streaming services to watch films and TV programmes in another language with subtitles to help. We can join chat groups or video calls with native speakers, we can watch the news in our target language. There is bound to be something that suits your preferred way of learning.

If anything, there is now too much information washing over us. To cut through the noise we need much more targeted attention – that is why it helps to have specific learning goals.

BUILD YOUR LEARNING ECOSYSTEM

Next, we dip our toes in the water and start to build a platform for accessing the relevant knowledge out there in a way that suits the way we want to learn. Take the topic you would like to learn more about and spend a little bit of time researching.

- Read the top ten blogs or articles that come up on search on the topic, summarize the key points and any other sources of information or people they refer to

- Search for books on the topic, read their descriptions to see which are the most credible, read a couple of them, then follow up any ideas or themes that look interesting

- Search on YouTube for TED Talks or videos from experts on the subject

- If it is an intellectual topic, try searching to see if there are any good academic papers or researchers

- Look on LinkedIn and Twitter to see who are the credible people specializing in this topic. Visit their feeds or websites and follow them

- Look online to see if there are any virtual or physical groups dedicated to discussing this topic

You might want to subscribe to any of the blogs, videos or online communities you find and follow people who are interesting in this area. Choose the media, pace and depth that work for you. If you follow people in a specific topic area on social media, then you have the added benefit that posts on that topic will regularly pop up on your feeds and keep adding to your learning. As always, be careful who you give this privilege to as they are capturing some of your attention – always be careful about who you let inside your head.

As a useful thought experiment, imagine you had the opportunity to spend a month with a world expert in any topic of your choice. Who would it be and what would you ask them to teach you? If you cannot make that happen in real life, you still have an opportunity to see them speak, read their books or follow their opinions online.

Remember, not all information is equal. The considered opinion of an expert in the field, an academic or professional writer, is certainly worth more than an unsubstantiated assertion by a stranger on social media. Focus on quality sources of information. If you come across controversial views, search to see if they are shared by another credible source.

As you read, listen and watch – be active by making notes or summaries of what you are learning. Look for ways to connect the new with what you already know as this will build the learning into a framework based on sound foundations. This helps you build an ecosystem of knowledge, tapping into people who have already spent considerable time and effort researching this very subject and amplifying your curiosity with theirs.

You can also opt to join a course of formal education such as the Open University or go back into an educational institution if this catches your imagination.

NOW REFLECT AND BRING YOUR OWN MEANING

For some people, just understanding something intellectually is enough, but even then you can reinforce your understanding of the topic by reflecting on it and bringing your own sense of organization and meaning to it.

As you get more into a subject, take the time to step back and organize your thoughts. What are the main themes you are coming across? Where are you most interested in, where do you want to go deeper or broader? Are there areas that do not interest you or where you feel you know enough?

You will find that the more you learn, the more nuances you can identify in the topic you are interested in. As your understanding becomes more granular you will see new angles to pursue or discard and you will get better at seeing how things fit together. Do not be afraid to refine your learning goal based on this new level of understanding.

One thing that always worked well for me in my research was to look for too much consensus. If everyone is saying the same thing or quoting the same research, it may be that everyone is just copying from the same source. Take a moment to search whether there is evidence that the opposite is true.

For example, in my leadership training practice, every time I researched a topic such as management, communication, collaboration or almost anything the consensus seemed to be that the answer was more teamwork and more communication. I spent time researching and thinking about the question, 'What if teamwork and communication is the problem, not the solution?' and it led me to develop some useful insights on asynchronous working and disconnecting from unnecessary cooperation, meetings and communication. This gave me a much more nuanced understanding of when collaboration was good and when it got in the way.

We have a saying in the training industry that if you really want to understand something, you should try training somebody else in it. You need to understand something well to explain it clearly to someone else. You could try sharing your new knowledge with friends or on forums.

This was part of my motivation in writing the book – by organizing the material in a way that other people could understand it helped me understand it better. By sharing ideas like this and learning about the different perspectives of our participants and readers in our training programmes, I can continue to learn and develop even better techniques and insights.

You can do this on your own by writing about a topic. Summarize what you have learned and what it means and detail how you could use this knowledge or information in a practical setting.

For some topics this might be enough, but it can be even more stimulating to apply your learning in the real world through joining a club, practising a skill or engaging with other people who share the interest.

Deliberate learning

For many physical skills we learn by doing, but simple repetition is not the best way to learn even these tasks. We can move up the learning curve more quickly by focusing on deliberate learning.

Malcolm Gladwell's book *Outliers: The Story of Success* famously proposed that it takes 10,000 hours of practice to become great at something. Subsequent researchers found that deliberate practice can explain 26 per cent of the variance between individuals in games performance, 21 per cent for music and 18 per cent for sports. It had negligible impact, however, on educational or professional performance.

Deliberate practice has two parts:

- practising with a specific goal in mind

- then spending time on feedback, thinking and reflection on what you have been doing.

As you start your learning journey, build in time for reflection and feedback after you have practised a physical skill. Consider what you learned and how you can apply it.

NOW APPLY IT

If it is a practical skill or sport, you are going to need to practise it if you want to get good at it. If it is something that requires other people, you will need to engage with a community, a class or a friend. If it is knowledge, you will need to do something with it to really embed the learning. You could read books and watch videos on some topics, such as dancing, for hours, but until you give it a try you have not really learned anything.

Where can you apply your new knowledge or skill? How and when will you begin?

Do not be discouraged by the fact that other people are better at whatever you are learning than you are. Someone will always be further along the journey than you, probably because they started before you did. Do not envy their knowledge or skill, be grateful that you can learn from them about their experiences and successes.

A true enthusiast will always be keen to share what they have learned with a newcomer. Learning is never finished – there is no complete or perfect learning.

LEARN TO FAIL FASTER AND BE HAPPY ABOUT IT

We rarely learn something worthwhile without failing at some point along the way. Some organizations like the music streaming service Spotify are even looking at ways to accelerate the rate at which they fail because this means they are learning faster. They also recognize that being afraid to fail or covering up that failure gets in the way of learning.

Carol Dweck, an American psychologist, studied students' attitudes about failure and proposed that people have underlying beliefs about learning and intelligence because of their mindset. She proposed the idea of fixed and growth mindsets. When we adopt a growth mindset, we act on the belief that our skills and intelligence can be improved through our efforts. We embrace challenges, overcome difficulties and learn from others and from our mistakes and feedback.

Fixed mindset	Growth mindset
I cannot do it	I am still learning
I am no good at that	How can I learn to get better at it?
It is too hard	With more practice it will get easier
I hate to make mistakes	Mistakes are how I learn and get better
Other people are better than I am at this	What can I learn from them?
I do not know how	Where can I learn how?
I cannot make this any better	I can always improve
I give up	I will try a different way
I am not smart enough	This may take some time and effort
I try to avoid challenges	I seek out challenges so I can learn
It puts me off that other people are better than me at this	I am inspired by other people's successes

Unsurprisingly, a growth mindset delivers better results and helps us to learn faster, be more creative, be more resilient, cope with change better and gain energy. Observe the language you use inside your head when you are learning things or facing new challenges and work to adopt a growth mindset.

Seeking flow in learning

In Chapter 4, we explained the concept of flow, that state where you are in the zone, focused and productive. Flow is a magnet for learning and makes for excellence in life. If you find yourself getting into a flow state where time passes and you did not even notice – keep going. If you find something boring, look for another media, or even another topic. Trust your instincts and follow your energy.

A flow state is characterized by moments of high challenge where you are exercising your skills at an elevated level:

- Where do your challenges currently exceed your skills (the goals where you try but often fail or have given up)?

- Where do your skills exceed the challenges you face (where you rarely feel stretched)?

To increase the possibility of flow occurring in these areas:

- if your skills exceed your goals, seek more challenge

- if your challenges exceed your skills, learn new skills.

It really can be as simple as that. By doing this systematically you create a positive spiral of seeking out new challenges and building new skills.

ENGAGE MULTIPLE LEARNING STYLES
There are various models and theories of learning styles. They propose that some people prefer to learn for example by theory or through practice; others prefer verbal learning or physical learning; some like to learn socially and some to reflect alone.

In general, these theories have been found to be too simplistic; we may have a relative preference, but most of us can benefit from engaging a full range of learning styles. Rich learning engages the whole mind and body in an active process, which happens on many levels at the same time.

When you are designing your own learning, build in activities that appeal to all the senses, that allow time in solitary reflection and in sharing things with others, that help you build a theoretical understanding and give you a chance to apply your learning. For most people, focusing on one single learning style is not as effective.

LEARNING TO KEEP UP TO DATE WITH TECHNOLOGY

I watched a street interview during the COVID-19 lockdowns in the UK with a woman who looked to be in her early 50s. The interviewer asked her how she was getting on with the new National Health Service COVID app which was required to access some services and to prove your vaccination status. 'Oh no,' she replied, 'I cannot be doing with any of those apps and online services at all.' At the age of 50 she had rejected the idea of ever being able to use an online system. Can you imagine how much in life she is already excluded from and how limited her options will be in 30 years' time?

Technology skills today are as important as driving or reading – if you cannot navigate the internet or use the host of apps that enable you to access services, book tickets, run your central heating and a thousand other things then you are already excluded from many options and aspects of life.

Depending on your age you may be able to look back at the technology of the past. If you can, think about what technology was able to do 30 years ago. Now try to imagine what it will be like 30 years from now. We have no real idea, but it is likely to include combinations of augmented reality, quantum computing, autonomous vehicles, the Internet of Things, personalized healthcare, smart homes and artificial intelligence. All aspects of our lives are likely to be influenced by these developments.

We do not need to be able to understand all the technology or learn to build the systems or write the code that makes it work (unless we want to). In the same way, we do not need to understand everything about our car to drive it (and we will not even need to know how to do that in 20 years' time), but we will need to know how to use technology to stay up to date and benefit from the advances that will undoubtedly come.

Let us start at a much more basic level.

- Do you know how to use the technology you have already got?

- Can you use all the functions of your TV controls?

- Do you know how to use the most useful features of the word processing or spreadsheet tools you use (or are you still using the functionality you picked up when you first learned these tools)?

- Do you understand how to use all the entertainment options in your car?

- Can you use all the useful functionality of your smartphone?

I appreciate that for many younger readers these will seem laughably simple. But be honest, as an example, if you use Microsoft Excel at work, do you know how to write a macro or do a regression analysis on a column of data? These are both incredibly useful and if you do not know how to do it then you have already fallen into this trap.

If you can answer these questions today, that is great. The challenge is in keeping up with the rate of change as the years go by. Will you be able to say the same when you are 60 or 90?

Science fiction writer Arthur C. Clarke once said, 'Any sufficiently advanced technology is indistinguishable from magic.' The technology you take for granted at the age of 20 may feel like magic to those over 70. Given the acceleration in technological change that is already happening, it will be a challenge to stay up to date.

Even as I am writing this, the press is filled with stories about the launch of the AI chatbot ChatGPT 4 and its planned integration into all Microsoft products and the introduction of Bard to Google Search. This looks set to revolutionize the use of all software and search. It is something all of us are going to need to keep learning about.

Take a walk around your house and ask yourself if you are really getting the best out of the devices you already own or if you are using basic functionality when a little bit of knowledge could allow you to get more out of them. You may need to set up your own tech support route (not always your kids), someone you can call if you have problems.

For everyday technology questions you can be sure there is a YouTube video explaining how you do it. I was talking to a client recently who had a problem with Microsoft Teams that she 'had been struggling with for weeks'. While we were talking, I searched on the question and found 1.3 million pages on how to solve it. It can take a bit of perseverance but there is an exceptionally good chance you can solve most basic problems this way.

Pick one technology problem you have faced with your devices at home. Try searching for the answer on your favourite search engine. If that does not work, try asking a question on the manufacturer's website, support forum or help page.

Get into the habit of not giving up on technology and actively searching for answers. If you do not, you will inevitably become out of date and this will really matter to the quality of your life in the future.

I hope I have motivated you to see learning as a key part of your strategy to continuously change and improve your life. Learning equips you with the tools to get from where you are today to where you want to be. Continuous learning also maintains brain health, stimulates curiosity and helps you stay up to date and relevant as you age.

Please see learning as an important element of living a good life, but also as an important part of delivering change in all the other areas of life. If you think you are done learning, take the advice of Apple's Steve Jobs: learn continually. There is always 'one more thing' to learn.

CHAPTER 9

Health and Financial Wellbeing

● ● ●

There are two essential elements of living a good life that I want to recognize but we are not going to cover in any detail: health and financial wellbeing. Both are important, but I decided not to focus on them in any detail for three main reasons:

1. The basics are simple and well known.

2. The subjects have been extensively covered elsewhere.

3. Beyond the basics it is better to get expert advice (and I am not an expert in these areas).

The challenge in these three areas is usually not a lack of knowledge but a lack of action. Both require long-term discipline and sacrifice, and it is easy to prioritize short-term spending and pleasure.

Every health and financial decision you make is an investment in the wellbeing of your future self. The money you spend today is not available for your retirement; your decision today to overeat or neglect exercise or your mental health will have an impact on your quality of life in the future.

Health

When I developed training modules on supporting mental and physical health for our clients during the COVID-19 lockdowns I struggled to find things to say that people did not already know. There cannot be many people who do not know the basics of living a healthy life:

- Get 7–8 hours' sleep per night.

- Do at least three sessions of exercise, adding up to at least 150 minutes of moderate aerobic activity or 75 minutes of vigorous aerobic activity, a week.

- Include at least two strength training sessions per week.

- Move more often, walk, take the stairs.

- Eat a balanced diet – a Mediterranean diet seems to work best for most people.

- Maintain a healthy weight.

- Do not smoke or take drugs; drink in moderation.

- Learn to cope with stress.

- Get professional medical advice for anything serious.

If, like most of us, you know these principles but do not routinely follow them, focus on building healthy habits in these areas first. Use Chapter 10 on action planning to include these in your life plan and improve the likelihood of you achieving your goals. Willpower alone is rarely enough.

It has never been easier to track and measure this accurately. Free or inexpensive apps and exercise trackers can tell us how many calories we are using, whether we have a healthy balanced diet, how much exercise we are taking and how to improve. We can bring a personal trainer into our living room on video or through apps at the touch of a button.

Do these basic (if difficult) things first and once you have, you may want to seek out specialist books and advice on diet and exercise, talk to a nutritionist or book a fitness consultation.

Many of the other topics in the book are designed to help you build more meaning, happiness and balance into your life. These are associated with higher levels of physical and mental wellbeing, lower stress and increased health and longevity.

Financial wellbeing

It is a similar story with achieving financial wellbeing. It is simple in principle and hard to follow in practice. You already know you need to:

- have a financial plan and goals

- spend less than you earn

- set a budget and monitor your spending

- build a reserve so unexpected bills do not throw you into debt

- invest any surplus in assets that will give you income later and keep doing that every month – regular savings and compound interest are the secret to success; once your passive income from assets exceeds your outgoings, you win

- avoid expensive debt, particularly credit cards – pay this off first

- get good advice on finance once you can afford it; once you are doing well, tax will probably be your biggest expense

- understand you generally do not get rich from salary – your own business, stock and investments are more reliable sources of real wealth.

Given improvements in longevity and healthcare it makes sense for most people, certainly those below middle age, to plan to have a 100-year life. A useful resource for thinking about this is Lynda Gratton and Andrew Scott's book *The 100 Year Life: Living and Working in an Age of Longevity*. As a mindset this does change your perspective on health and finances. A good rule of thumb is that you need about 25 times more than your annual costs to retire (this assumes a 4 per cent yield on your investment).

As with health, implement these principles first.

Once you can generate a surplus above your everyday expenses, then it is time to save. If you cannot generate a surplus, you need either to increase your income (get a better paying position or additional jobs) or reduce your outgoings. I realize this sounds simplistic or even brutal, and I know this can be difficult, but there really is no other way out of living from hand to mouth financially.

Remember that every choice you make regarding health and finance defines the quality of life of your future self, for the rest of your life. Success in both areas requires taking a long-term view and modifying our shorter-term behaviours to produce longer-term gains.

What advice would your 100-year-old self like to give you about your spending, saving, eating and exercise habits today?

CHAPTER 10

Planning Your Happiness

* * *

As you have completed the exercises in this book you should have developed some concrete ideas on how to build a happier and more fulfilling life. These could drive a lot of changes in your life, some small, some hopefully life-altering. This chapter is about how to turn your ideas into actions and habits and overcome the most common barriers to change.

Contrary to popular opinion, people love change. Who would not want to have lost weight, learned a language or a musical instrument, found their perfect job? The difficult bit is doing the work needed to get to the final state – all these changes require sustained effort and sometimes taking a risk.

In this chapter, I will introduce some tools and techniques to help you in planning and navigating your journey in six key areas:

1. Being clear about your direction.

2. Setting goals that are more likely to work.

3. Finding the time.

4. Managing the journey.

5. Keeping on track.

6. Bringing others with you.

I often say on our training courses that all the value is in the application, the work you do to implement the ideas you've had. As the American author and educator Stephen Covey says, 'To know and not do is not really knowing.'

1 Being clear about your direction

To begin implementing our desired future life, we need to identify our direction of travel. We have covered a lot of ground in this book and you should now have a whole range of ideas about changes you would like to make across different areas of your life.

I would encourage you to think about your journey as a direction rather than a fixed destination. If you head in the direction you want, you will learn things and be able to adapt and evolve as you go. True engagement and happiness are about enjoying the moment and the journey rather than obsessing about an idealized future.

There is an insightful book called *Build Your Future Self Now* by Dr Josh Hardy. It is worth a read, but the book title gives you the basic message. The idea is that if you can vividly envisage the self you want to be in the future, you create an impetus that pulls you towards that future. Once you are clear about this direction there are lots of things you can start doing right now to make the likelihood of that future happening much higher.

Think about the person you were 10 or 20 years ago – your perspectives, circumstances and priorities were quite different. You should expect a similar level of change going forward. Because of this it is hard to image how you will be in 20 or 50 years – we usually underestimate future changes.

Start by visualizing your future life as you want to be at some point in the medium-term future, say 5–10 years from now:

• How will your life be?

• What will you be doing?

• Where will you be?

• Who will you be with?

• How does it feel?

• What will your typical day look and feel like?

Write all this down.

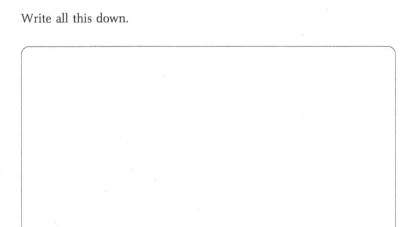

Try to make it as vivid as possible. Without a compelling future vision, we tend to be driven either by short-term goals or by avoiding current pains and problems.

It can be hard to identify with ourselves in the far future, which is why people tend not to save enough for retirement. We can help counter this by making our future vision of ourselves as real and impactful as possible. Then work backwards, halving the time from now to your desired future. If your original vision was for 10 years from now, set yourself goals for five years, then two and a half years, 15 months, etc., right down to the next few weeks and the day. Ask yourself, how can you either start to live this way right now or put in place the stepping stones over time that will get you there?

Everything you do is an investment in your future self: the money you save today will bring about a more comfortable life for your future self; the food you eat today will have an impact on the health and fitness of your future self. Every major decision you make, both good and bad, has implications for the quality of your future life.

What will your future self think about the decisions you are making today? What will they wish you had been doing differently?

To bring your future self into the present, when you are facing a big decision or simply reflecting on your life, ask yourself, 'How would my future self behave if they had the opportunity to come back and live this day?', 'What would they do or decide in this situation?'.

Now is a good time to stop doing things that do not lead in the direction of a successful and healthy future self.

2 Setting goals that are more likely to work

We all know we need to set goals if we want to get something done, but we rarely do it in a systematic way. All our actions are goal-oriented in some way, otherwise we would not do anything. However, if our goals are not clear or are too small, we will act accordingly. It is better if our goals are clear and stretching.

PRIORITIZE

Now is a suitable time to bring together all your ideas, thoughts and intentions from reading this book.

Go back to your objectives for making these changes. What is it you are trying to achieve? What will really make you more fulfilled and happier in life?

A useful way of prioritizing and deciding where to start is to categorize your ideas on an impact versus difficulty grid. How much impact will achieving this goal have on moving you towards your objectives and how difficult will making the change be?

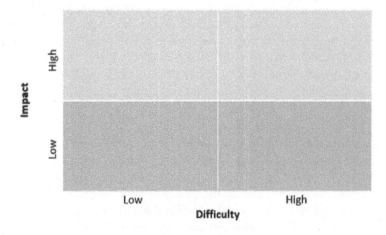

If you have things that are high impact and low difficulty, then it makes sense to do these first and get some quick wins under your belt.

Major changes are often high impact and high difficulty and you will need to break these into smaller steps and work on them systematically over time. Do not put them off just because they are difficult, allocate time to keep moving them forward.

Low-impact, low-difficulty changes are not really moving you forward, but it can be satisfying to tick a few easy things off your list; just make sure you are not staying busy with things that do not really make a substantial difference. Things that have a minimal impact but take a lot of effort you may want to prioritize last, or even reconsider whether they are worth doing.

STOP, START, MORE, LESS

Another useful prioritization and planning tool is to think about four categories of activities and how you spend your time:

- What will I **stop** doing? When we make a change, we often just think about adding on more things we need to do, but we should also stop doing some existing things to make more time to work on the new, or just because they are not moving us towards our new goal.

- What will I **start** doing? Are there new things you need to begin that you have not done in the past?

- What will I **do less** of? These are things you do not want to stop doing entirely but you do want to spend less time on, such as passively watching TV.

- What will I **do more** of? These are things you enjoy and want to make more time for in your future life.

SET SMART+ GOALS

Setting SMART goals means that each of your goals should be:

- Specific – not 'I want to do more exercise' but 'I will exercise three times a week for a minimum of 45 minutes'. Do be careful however when you are making plans to change lots of things that a specific goal in one area does not conflict with your overall goal of improving your life in total.

- Measurable – you are more likely to achieve your goal if there is a measure associated with it, such as the three times a week clause above. If you visually and publicly track your progress against these measures, you are more likely to stay on track. In the exercise example this might be by having a tick sheet on your fridge door.

- Achievable – goals should be achievable, but people are more likely to achieve goals that are a bit challenging rather than too easy.

- Relevant – goals should have meaning to you and your life.

- Time bounded – they should have dates and steps attached to them rather than just being an open-ended intention.

Other good advice on goal setting:

- Do not be too focused on your final objective or end goal, particularly if it is a major change. Instead focus on achieving the next step on your journey. Continuous improvement and smaller quick wins are more motivating and more likely to keep you moving forward.

- Celebrating your achievements is a good motivator to continue, so remember to include some reward and recognition for meeting your goals.

The language of goals is important. When we say we 'should' do something, this implies obligation and an external standard, or another person telling you that you ought to do it. As we have learned already, external motivations are much weaker than internal or intrinsic ones. 'Should' also frames the goal as a possibility, not a certainty; there is some reluctance built into the word – I should exercise more.

Use more positive language for your goals. Phrases like 'I will', 'I plan', 'I choose to', 'I can' state you have freely chosen this course of action and intend to follow it. Language does matter.

In working with this idea myself I have learned to make words like 'must' or 'have to' triggers for me to stop for a moment and think about why I am really doing something. If on reflection it is something I am doing only because someone else thinks it is important, then it is unlikely I am really going to do it. If it is important, I consciously change my language to 'I choose to ...', 'It does make a difference'.

3 Finding the time

Inevitably when we start to do something new, we ask ourselves, 'How will I find the time to do this given all the other things in my life?' Sometimes this is a real problem, but sometimes, if we are honest with ourselves, it is just an excuse for not putting the effort in.

Time is a zero-sum game; an hour you spend on one activity is an hour less to spend on another, so spending your time in pursuit of the life you want is all about prioritizing. You already have all the time you will ever get. In each week everyone has the same 168 hours, what we can influence is how we choose to spend them.

Most people spend an average of 8 hours per night sleeping (56 hours per week), leaving 112 waking hours. How do you spend those hours on each of the areas of a good life?

Area	How many hours do you spend on this per week?	Percentage of your 112 waking hours
Work		
Engaging leisure and interests		
Positive relationships		
Lifelong learning		
Physical and mental health and wellbeing		
Financial wellbeing		

You might need to keep a diary for a while to work this out accurately, but you should have a broad idea when thinking about a typical week. If you are in full-time work, this is likely to take about 40 hours, leaving 72 hours to allocate as you see fit. In Chapter 7 we looked extensively at how people typically spend their leisure time. Most people are spending between 25 per cent and 40 per cent of their waking time in leisure, and we identified a particular opportunity to replace passive leisure with more active pursuits. Go back and review your thoughts from that chapter.

Based on the ideas you have generated throughout the book, plan how you will allocate your time in future to achieve your goals.

Area	How many hours will you spend on this per week?	Percentage of your 112 waking hours
Work		
Engaging leisure and interests		
Positive relationships		
Lifelong learning		
Physical/mental health and wellbeing		
Financial wellbeing		

YOUR TIME IS YOUR SCARCEST RESOURCE AND THE QUALITY OF YOUR LIFE IS HOW YOU SPEND YOUR HOURS

Where can you cut out things that are not a priority or do not move you closer to your future you? What activities would more closely match your new priorities?

If you still think you do not have the time, set yourself a small target, say spending 30 minutes a day less watching TV or staring at your phone, and use that time to do something more productive. If that works for you, try the next 30 minutes.

At the end of the day, the choices you make about how you spend your time are decisions about the quality of your life. You always have choices and each choice brings consequences. Nobody else can do this for you.

A slight change really adds up. Let us say you are age 40 with a life expectancy of another 45 years. Imagine if you could spend just 5 per cent more of your waking hours on things you enjoy instead of things you do not. That adds up to 5.5 hours per week, 286 hours per year, 11,440 hours or two years of more positive experience in your life, and do not forget the two years of negative things you stopped doing to make the space.

Surely it is possible to make a 5 per cent improvement in anything, and if so, why not 10 per cent?

One of my favourite maxims is believed to come originally from Hillel, a first-century Jewish scholar, and has been used subsequently by inspirational speakers like John Lewis and John F Kennedy: 'If not you, then who; if not now, then when?'

START WITH AN EMPTY DIARY

Given that time is usually our scarcest resource, how would you choose to spend your time if you had a completely empty diary and started again with planning your week from zero?

Begin with an empty week planner and populate your week, starting with your highest priorities, the things that give you meaning and happiness. Make sure you are allocating time for them first. Once your week is full, if you do not get round to doing other things you would like to, then only your lowest priorities will suffer. If you have commitments you really cannot avoid, such as work, schedule them in first, then focus on building your priorities, in order, into the rest of your waking time.

In a busy life we can often fall into the trap of doing the urgent things rather than the important ones. Time pressure is one of the great excuses, but everyone has the same number of hours – successful people just use their time differently. It is up to you how you will spend your time.

TREAT MONEY THE SAME WAY AS TIME

For most of us the other scarce resource is money and a common objection or excuse to making a change is that we cannot afford it.

As with time, there is an opportunity cost for everything. We can choose to go out and exchange more of our time for more money by working longer or find ways to increase our value and earning potential. But even with more wealth, the money we spend on one thing is not available to spend on something else that might be more enjoyable or useful or might move us closer to our goals. We need to prioritize.

Evaluate how you are spending your money currently and how you would like to spend it to make your life more engaging and happier. Think about what you need to stop and start spending on and where you would like to spend more, or less. What can you afford that moves you in the direction of your dream?

4 Managing the journey

Managing the journey from where you are now to where you want to be is often a major challenge. Willpower is rarely enough, so here are some tips and ideas about how you can support your journey and make it more likely to succeed:

- Create an environment that makes change inevitable.

- Use learning as the fuel.

- Move from fear of failure to constant experiments.

- Adopt a growth mindset.

- Follow your energy.

- Build new habits – start tiny.

- Break some patterns.

- Do not keep investing in past mistakes.

CREATE AN ENVIRONMENT THAT MAKES CHANGE INEVITABLE

When we try to make a change, we often rely on willpower alone and for major changes this is usually not enough. We are usually more successful if we create an environment around us that makes the change inevitable or makes it hard for us to fall off the path we have set for ourselves.

This involves managing our environment, external cues, rewards and social context to make the change easier and remove any elements that get in the way of the change. For example, if you want to get fitter, instead of just setting a goal (which is a good start but relies on will-power), think how you could engineer an environment that makes this inevitable.

You can change your weekly shop to cut out unhealthy products, purge your fridge of unhealthy options, use an app to track your diet and activity levels, join a gym, get some home exercise equipment, enrol in a class, set an alarm on your phone to go for a walk each day, read books about health and exercise, tell friends what you are trying to do, spend more time with friends who are healthy and less with the couch potatoes, publish your target and have a progress sheet visible on your fridge door, walk to work or park your car half a mile away to finish the journey on foot, get a balance chair, have walking meetings.

You can produce dozens of other ideas – what works best depends on your preferences. The mindset is, 'How can I design my total environment so that the change I want is inevitable?'

You can also change your internal environment by improving your inputs and mindset. Learn about techniques to get you where you want to go, meet inspiring people (online or in person), think deeply, experiment. If you change your inputs, your outputs will start to change automatically. What new inputs would support your change? How can you design a mindset that supports the change you want?

What is your goal?	What external environment would support this?	What new inputs would help?

USE LEARNING AS THE FUEL

You made a great start on acquiring the learning you need to change your life by buying this book. Continuing to learn will give you more tools and inspiration to continue with the journey.

If you have been inspired by any of the topics in the book, then take the next step and read more deeply into these areas. See Chapter 8 for ideas on how to use your curiosity and desire to change to fuel your continuing transformation. What do you need to learn to support achieving your goal?

FROM FEAR OF FAILURE TO CONSTANT EXPERIMENTS THAT CANNOT FAIL

Another common barrier to change is our fear of failure. This stops us ever getting started or makes us give up when things get tough.

The future is never real until it becomes the present, so all our concerns for the future are imaginary. Our minds are excellent at creating imaginary futures and are much more sensitized to imagining the negatives than the positives. A good question to ask is, 'What's the worst that could happen?' In most instances the realistic worst is not as bad as your imagination can make it seem.

When you are trying something new, it is useful to think of everything as an experiment. In an experiment we develop an idea, try it and learn if it works. If you see everything in terms of binary success or failure, then sometimes you fail.

However, if you see everything as an experiment, with the goal of learning, then however it turns out, you win – you will have learned whether it works for you or not. If it did not work, you now have more information to design your next experiment, which will be more likely to succeed because you have learned more about yourself and the situation.

. Remember, for a successful experiment you must be clear about why you were trying something and you also must collect information and learning that will tell you whether it worked. If it did not work, you use this information to design your next experiment.

What is the next experiment you plan to try? What would you like to learn from it?

ADOPT A GROWTH MINDSET

In Chapter 8 I introduced you to Carol Dweck's concept of the growth mindset, where we act on the belief that our skills and intelligence can be improved through our own efforts. Go back and review this idea in the context of constructing your change journey. Are you approaching this with a growth mindset? If not, how can you do so?

FOLLOW YOUR ENERGY

During my own coaching and reading on this subject I learned to focus more on following my energy. If something gives you energy, makes you feel engaged and increases happiness, you feel it in your body. You feel lighter, more optimistic and more energetic. You are approaching the task, person or situation eagerly and with anticipation. If something subtracts energy or makes you feel unhappy, you feel it in your stomach, in the tension in your shoulders, in your reluctance to continue. You may drag your feet as you approach it.

These are extreme examples, but it is worthwhile learning to monitor yourself and your reactions to things. What gives you energy and what takes it away? What are the physical reactions you feel when something is not going well? Notice how you feel in various places, at different times of day and with different people. If you feel tension or reluctance, pause and try to identify what is changing your energy level.

Many emotions evolved to motivate us to do something differently or to reach out for something we are lacking. In the same way as hunger motivates us to eat, loneliness is meant to motivate us to reach out and find the companionship we are lacking, and boredom is a motivator to seek out more variety. Treat these emotions as useful signals – do not wallow in them but realize they are a prompt to do something differently.

The principle is simple: follow your energy, do more of what gives you energy and do less of what reduces your energy.

What gives me energy and how could I do more of that?	What reduces my energy and how could I do less of that?

If you do this one thing consciously and regularly it will make an enormous difference to the quality of your experience.

BUILD NEW HABITS – START TINY

Embedding change means setting new habits. If we must think about everything as we do it, it becomes exhausting. If we can make new habits part of our everyday routines and simple to incorporate, then change is much more likely to stick.

In his book *Tiny Habits*, B J Fogg gives some practical advice on establishing new habits:

1. Behaviour change requires motivation – be clear about why you are doing it.

2. Make the habit tiny to begin with – take the first step by establishing a habit so small it is easy. If you want to learn to do 100 press-ups, start by doing 1. As you get into the routine of doing one press-up every day you will find yourself naturally doing two, then ten. The important thing is to do something every day until it becomes a habit.

3. It requires ability – are you able to do it? If you are not currently able to deliver the change then focus on learning and practice or getting the right tools and equipment. If something is hard to do, find ways to make it easier – automate it, get organized or start with a minor change that is easier to implement.

4. Set a prompt to remind you to exercise the change. The best prompts are links to existing behaviour or events that are already embedded. The prompt should be in the same place where you want to exhibit the new behaviour and of similar frequency and character, so it does not require you to fundamentally change location or state.

Fogg suggests using the format 'when I ..., I will ...':

- When I first sit down at my desk, I will work on my #1 priority for 30 minutes before looking at emails.

- When I make a cup of tea, I will stand up and make a sales call or do three press-ups.

- Before I eat lunch, I will take a ten-minute walk.

Start small and embed the habit. Once it is working you can scale it up if needed.

Remember to celebrate success when you do it:

- What habits do you want to implement?

- What is the smallest step you could start with?

- How can you raise your motivation to change?

- How can you make it easier to do?

- How can you link it to a prompt or trigger behaviour that you already do?

You can also use this in reverse to get rid of unhealthy habits. Choose a habit you want to change, remove the prompt, make it harder to do or reduce your motivation or ability to do it.

DO NOT KEEP INVESTING IN PAST MISTAKES

The 'sunk cost fallacy' is where people are reluctant to stop doing something or continue to invest more time and effort into something, even when they should not, just because they have put so much effort in already. It is particularly common in financial decisions where people have invested in a business or a new activity and it is not working. They should stop, but because they have spent so much money already, they choose to invest more in the hope that it will improve.

The 'sunk cost' is the time, effort and money you have put into something in the past. The reality is that this has now gone and usually cannot be recovered. You should make the right decision at this moment, based on what leads you towards your future self, even if that means abandoning some aspects of your previous life you have worked hard on.

Let us be honest, that can be extremely hard to do. For example, you might have put a lot of effort into learning skills you do not enjoy exercising or into a career that is making you miserable. It feels as though you have worked so hard that you should keep doing it. But sometimes you must stop and consider all that effort to be in the past and starting from today think about what is the right course of action for the rest of your life.

Do not keep doing the wrong thing for your future just because your past self chose to invest in it –the past is gone. You can shape your own future, but only by the actions you take in the present.

BREAK YOUR PATTERNS

I have a high need for variety and a particular horror of routine and following rules. I need to change things just for the sake of it. You might want to, too.

It is easy in life to fall into routines and these routines can limit our options. When we do something in a routine way, we tend to fall back into autopilot mode and not really experience the moment. You may experience this when you drive to a place you have not been before and suddenly you must pay more attention to your surroundings.

I like to introduce variety just for its own sake and a good place to start is to look at any patterns you have fallen into and just do something different. This might be as small as taking a different route to work or as big as moving to another country.

Where are your opportunities for everyday rebellion and deviance from your norm? What patterns have you fallen into and how can you break these patterns on purpose? You may learn that your old patterns are fine and go back to the way you have always done things, but you may find something new.

If you really want to mix things up, here is an exercise inspired by the cult novel *The Dice Man* by Luke Rhinehart where the protagonist gives over full control of his life to the roll of the dice.

When you are faced with a choice such as what to read, where to eat or where to visit, start by producing a list of six options – choose six books, six restaurants or six locations. Make a numbered list. Include some of the types of options you would typically choose but add in one that would be a stretch for you, and at least one option that is outside your comfort zone. Then roll the dice and whichever one comes up is the one you must do.

In the novel the protagonist gets carried away and includes immoral and criminal options – I do not suggest you do the same.

I travel around the world on business a lot and it is easy to fall back on ordering the food that I recognize. To prevent that tendency, I usually ask the local person sitting next to me to choose my meal. I do not give them any information about what I enjoy or dislike, I just ask them to order something that they would enjoy. It always prompts an interesting conversation about local cuisine and most people take the responsibility of finding me something tasty seriously. Very occasionally I get something I do not really like, but I nearly always get to try a local speciality that I would never have ordered myself.

What patterns will you break, just for the hell of it?

5 Keeping on track

It is not enough to set goals, we need to collect information on how they are going, review our progress and replan from time to time to keep us on track.

On several occasions in this book, I have encouraged you to keep a record of your experiences, the things you enjoy, the things you appreciate and want to savour, the things that give you energy, make you curious or bring flow at work. It is only by capturing this information regularly that we can continue to drive improvement. I find that a notes page on my phone is a practical way to do this as I always have my phone with me.

If we really want to meet our goals, we need to get into the habit of regular reviews and planning sessions. Here is our suggestion on a process of capturing and reviewing progress. If you find this too much, work out the schedule that fits your preferences.

Whatever works for you, now is the time to get your diary out and set some recurring appointments or alarms to remind you to do this.

Frequency	Examples
Daily – capture the moment as it happens or set a phone alarm to make a note of what happened today	What gave you joy? What changed your energy levels significantly? What were you curious about? What are you grateful for or will savour in the future? What did you enjoy or dislike?

Frequency	Examples
Weekly – reflect and replan: consider what happened this week and what you will do next week	What did you appreciate this week? Savour the top three positive experiences of the previous week. Plan your next acts of kindness. Plan how you can spend more time on the things you enjoyed and gave you energy and cut down on the things that brought your energy down.
Monthly progress check – how are you doing against your goals?	What progress have you made against your plan? What will you do next in each of the areas of building a better life?
3–6 monthly – longer reflection	Set aside some quiet time to reflect on how it is going and what you need to do to keep on track in your plan or update it.
5–10 years from now	Make a note to work through this book again in a few years as your life goals evolve.

6 Bringing others with you

In this book we have focused on you making the change you want. You cannot change others, you can only change yourself, so it makes sense to start with this. However, we all exist within a network of relationships, and making and sustaining change is hard without the understanding and support of the important people in your life.

You should certainly encourage your closest partner to read this book, work through the process for themselves and discuss your ideas. Whether they do or not, you need to discuss your learning and the changes you want to make. Some of these may need to be negotiated, some you can start doing on your own.

Social pressure will also help you achieve your goals. Your friends and family can give you support and help hold you to account, so tell them what your goals are – and be specific.

Will your plans fulfil your purpose?

We have come to the end of the book, but hopefully not the end of your process of planning and living an engaged and happy life.

Have you met your objectives?

Do you have a practical plan to live each of your values, exercise your key strengths, pursue your passions and achieve your purpose?

In a portfolio life and career, it is unlikely you will fulfil all of these through just one job or interest, but taken together, the range of activities you have planned should allow you to fulfil all these elements somewhere. If there are still gaps, dreams you want to pursue or values that you have not found a way to express, then go back over your plans to fill those gaps.

Do you have a plan in each of the key areas of living a good life that moves you in the direction of the future self you want to be?

It is tempting when you get to the end of a book to think 'that was interesting' and put it on the shelf, never to be seen again. I hope you will come back to this book regularly to get some ideas on making progress in the areas you are trying to improve. I hope you have enjoyed the process of reading the book, but it would be a real shame if you did not take some of the actions that could make a significant difference to the quality of your life.

You may find that your thinking on the themes in this book continues to develop for several months. As you start thinking differently and actively evaluating and planning your life you will learn new things about yourself and your plans may change. The important thing is to start. It is hard to overcome inertia, much easier to get going and then change direction if you need to.

What is your first experiment and when will you start?

I would love to hear what you tried and the impact it had on you and your life. You can contact me at support@yourportfoliolife.com

If you would like the opportunity to work on the themes in the book with expert trainers and coaches, we offer workshops, webinars and one-to-one coaching for individuals.

We also offer programmes for organizations or leaders who want to help their people find more purpose and engagement at work. See more about our corporate programmes at www.global-integration.com

Good luck in finding your purpose and building a better life and career.

Kevan Hall

Notes

* * *

Introduction

Gallup (2022) State of the Global Workplace Report: The Voice of the World's Employees.

Chapter 1

PwC (2018) UK Economic Outlook Report, 17 July.
William Bridges (1980) *Transitions: Making Sense of Life's Changes*, Hachette Books.

Chapter 2

Douglas Adams (2020) *The Hitchhiker's Guide to the Galaxy*, Pan.
Declaration of Independence, www.loc.gov/exhibits/declara/ruffdrft.html#:~:-text=We%20hold%20these%20truths%20to,governments%20are%20instituted%20among%20men%2C
Elizabeth Dunn and Michael Norton (2013) *Happy Money: The Science of Smarter Spending*, Oneworld Publications.
Elizabeth Dunn, Lara B Aknin and Michael I. Norton (2009) Prosocial spending and happiness: Using money to benefit others pays off, *Current Directions in Psychological Science*, 31(6), 536–545.
Bassam Khoury, Tania Lecomte, Guillaume Fortin, Marjolaine Masse, Phillip Therien, Vanessa Bouchard, Marie-Andrée Chapleau, Karine Paquin and Stefan G Hofmann (2013) Mindfulness-based therapy: A comprehensive meta-analysis, *Clinical Psychology Review*, 33(6), August, 763–771.
Sonja Lyubomirsky (2010) *The How of Happiness: A Scientific Approach to Getting the Life You Want*, Piatkus.
P Brickman and D T Campbell (1971) Hedonic relativism and planning the good society. In Mortimer H Appley (Ed.), *Adaptation-level Theory* (pp. 287–305), Academic Press.

Martin Seligman (2011) *Flourish: A New Understanding of Happiness and Well-being – And How to Achieve Them*, Nicholas Brealey Publishing.
Harvard Study of Adult Development, www.adultdevelopmentstudy.org/
Martin E P Seligman (2006) *Learned Optimism: How to Change Your Mind and Your Life*, Vintage Books.
Karmel Choi, www.health.harvard.edu/mind-and-mood/more-evidence-that-exercise-can-boost-mood
Mihaly Csikszentmihalyi (2008) *Flow: The Psychology of Optimal Experience*, Harper Perennial Modern Classics.
www.ons.gov.uk/peoplepopulationandcommunity/wellbeing/articles/measuring-nationalwellbeing/atwhatageispersonalwellbeingthehighest

Chapter 3

Steve Chamberlain (2020) *On Purpose: What Are You Really Here to Do?*, Nielsen.
Marcus Buckingham (2002) *Now, Discover Your Strengths: How to Develop Your Talents and Those of the People You Manage*, Free Press.
Howard Gardner (1993) *Frames of Mind: The Theory of Multiple Intelligences*, Basic Books.
www.mckinsey.com/capabilities/people-and-organizational-performance/our-insights/the-search-for-purpose-at-work

Chapter 4

Gallup (2022) State of the Global Workplace 2022 Report: The Voice of the World's Employees.
Mihaly Csikszentmihalyi (2008) *Flow: The Psychology of Optimal Experience*, Harper Perennial Modern Classics.
Adam Grant (2014) *Give and Take: Why Helping Others Drives Our Success*, Penguin Books.
The economic impact of artificial intelligence on the UK economy (pwc.co.uk) https://www.pwc.co.uk/economic-services/assets/ai-uk-report-v2.pdf
Randy Komisar and Kent L Lineback (2000) *The Monk and the Riddle: The Education of a Silicon Valley Entrepreneur*, Harvard Business Review Press.
www.futuremarketinsights.com/reports/employee-engagement-market#

Chapter 5

Charles Handy (2011) *The Empty Raincoat: Making Sense of the Future*, Cornerstone Digital.

Henry David Thoreau, www.brainyquote.com/quotes/henry_david_thoreau_106427

R Jason Faberman, Andreas I Mueller, Ayşegül Şahin, Rachel Schuh and Giorgio Topa, published 5 April 2017, How do people find jobs?, Liberyty Stret Econmics/New York Fed https://libertystreeteconomics.newyorkfed.org/2017/04/how-do-people-find-jobs/

The gig economy, www.mckinsey.com/featured-insights/mckinsey-explainers/what-is-the-gig-economy

https://www.statista.com/chart/18908/self-employed-workers-by-country/

Chapter 6

6% of adults in the UK always or often felt lonely, a further 19% felt lonely some of the time, UK Government Official Statistics Community Life Survey 2021/22: Wellbeing and loneliness, Community life survey 2021/22: Wellbeing and loneliness - GOV.UK (www.gov.uk)https://www.gov.uk/government/statistics/community-life-survey-202122/community-life-survey-202122-wellbeing-and-loneliness

Professor Robin Dunbar (2010) *How Many Friends Does One Person Need?: Dunbar's Number and Other Evolutionary Quirks*, Faber and Faber.

David L Bradford and Carole Robin (2022) *Connect: Building Exceptional Relationships with Family, Friends and Colleagues*, Penguin Life.

Max Dickins (2022) *Billy No-Mates: How I Realized Men Have a Friendship Problem*, Canongate Books.

Harvard Study of Adult Development, www.adultdevelopmentstudy.org/

Jeffrey A Hall (2018) How many hours does it take to make a friend?, *Journal of Social and Personal Relationships*, 36(4).

Chapter 7

www.marketwatch.com/story/retired-and-bored-or-worse-yet-boring-try-this-11649890423

www.finder.com/uk/tv-statistics

Catherine Price (2022) *The Power of Fun: Why Fun Is the Key to a Happy and Healthy Life*, Transworld Digital.

Mihaly Csikszentmihalyi (1998) *Finding Flow: The Psychology of Engagement with Everyday Life*, Basic Books.

Transamerica Center for Retirement Studies Report (2017) Global Retirement Aspirations.

Chapter 8

European Union Labour Force Survey 2022 https://ec.europa.eu/eurostat/
    statistics-explained/index.php?title=Adult_learning_statistics#:~:text=In%20
    2022%2C%20the%20proportion%20of%20persons%20aged%2025,the%20
    corresponding%20share%20in%202020%2C%20see%20Table%201.
Gandhi, https://ethology.eu/live-as-if-you-were-to-die-tomorrow-learn-as-if-you-
    were-to-live-forever/
Richard Harris, www.drsandrafolk.com/blog/it-all-starts-with-curiosity-how-to-
    ask-the-right-questions
Ellen Parr, https://quoteinvestigator.com/2015/11/01/cure/
Malcolm Gladwell (2009) *Outliers: The Story of Success*, Penguin.
Carol Dweck (2016) *Mindset: Changing the Way You Think to Fulfil Your Potential*,
    Little Brown Book Group.
https://en.wikipedia.org/wiki/Clarke%27s_three_laws
Steve Jobs quote: Learn continually - there's always 'one more thing' to learn!
    (azquotes.com)https://www.azquotes.com/quote/1060450

Chapter 9

Lynda Gratton and Andrew Scott (2016) *The 100-Year Life: Living and Working
    in an Age of Longevity*, Bloomsbury Information.

Chapter 10

Covey, S (1989) *The Seven Habits of Highly Effective People*, p. 12.
Dr Josh Hardy (2022) *Build Your Future Self Now: Secrets on how to be inten-
    tional about your future*, independently published.
B J Fogg (2020) *Tiny Habits: The small changes that change everything*, Virgin
    Books.
Luke Rhinehart (1999) *The Dice Man*, HarperCollins Publishers.

About the Author

* * *

Kevan Hall is a successful entrepreneur, writer and trainer who has spent the last 30 years as a keynote speaker and trainer working with many of the world's leading organizations.

After a successful career in major multinationals in the UK and France he founded Global Integration in 1994 with people based around the world and a mission to inspire and enable people to succeed in complex organizations.

He pioneered practical training in remote and hybrid working and matrix management. He is the author of books on leadership speed, matrix management, effective meetings, and remote and virtual working.

While working on training to improve employee engagement he became fascinated with how people find purpose and engagement at work. He realized that people spent 40 per cent of their working lives for 40 years at work and discovered that only 20 per cent of people said they were fully engaged at work. He felt this was a huge waste of both human potential and business productivity and resolved to do something about it.

This book and the associated training and coaching are the result.

Kevan is a keen football fan (Reading FC), traveller, scuba diver and motorsport enthusiast.

About Global Integration Training/Your Portfolio Life

* * *

Global Integration – services for leaders and organizations

Global Integration is an international training and consulting company working with major multinationals around the world in three key areas:

- matrix management

- remote, virtual and hybrid working

- finding purpose and engagement at work.

They provide highly interactive face-to-face and live web seminar training and online learning in these topics.

If you need the people in your team or organization to find a sense of purpose and engagement at work to improve productivity, retention and wellbeing, please contact us at www.global-integration.com to schedule a free introductory call with one of our specialists.

Your Portfolio Life – services for individuals

If you are an individual wanting to find your purpose in life and at work, and you would like to redesign the rest of your life, then YPL provides individual coaching and group programmes to help.

You can work with our expert coaches and join a group of other individuals on the same journey. Find out more at www.yourportfoliolife.com